Wisconsin Lighthouses

To our daughter Sarah Lacey, the "light" of our lives

Wisconsin Lighthouses

A Photographic & Historical Guide

Ken & Barb Wardius

Prairie Oak
PRESS

Madison, Wisconsin

First edition, second printing
Copyright © 2000 by Ken and Barb Wardius

Prairie Oak Press
821 Prospect Place
Madison, Wisconsin 53703

Designed by Flying Fish Graphics, Blue Mounds, Wisconsin

All photographs by the authors, unless otherwise indicated.
Front cover photo: Wind Point Lighthouse, Racine, WI
Back cover photo: Wisconsin Point Light, Superior, WI

Printed in Korea

        Library of Congress Cataloging-in-Publication Data

Wardius, Ken.
    Wisconsin lighthouses : a photographic & historical guide / Ken & Barb Wardius.--1st ed.
        p. cm.
    Includes bibliographical references and index.
    ISBN 1-879483-60-2
    1. Lighthouses--Wisconsin. I. Wardius, Barb. II. Title.

VK1024.W6 W37 2000
387. 1'55'09775--dc21
                                00-027514

Contents

Acknowledgments   vii

Note to the Reader   ix

Introduction   xi

Lake Superior   3

   Wisconsin Point Light   4

   Apostle Islands   6

     Sand Island Lighthouse   8

     Raspberry Island Lighthouse 10

     Devils Island Lighthouse   12

     Outer Island Lighthouse   14

     Michigan Island Old Lighthouse 17

     Michigan Island Light Tower 19

     La Pointe Lighthouse   21

     Chequamegon Point Light   23

   Ashland Breakwater Light   24

Lake Winnebago   27

     Neenah Lighthouse   28

     Asylum Bay Lighthouse   30

     Rockwell Lighthouse   32

     Fond du Lac Lighthouse   35

Lake Michigan   37

   Bay of Green Bay   38

     Menominee North Pier Light   39

     Green Island Lighthouse Ruins 41

     Peshtigo Reef Light   45

     Green Bay Harbor Entrance Light 46

     Long Tail Point Light Ruins 48

     Grassy Island Range Lights   49

   Door County   53

     Sherwood Point Lighthouse   54

     Chambers Island Lighthouse   57

     Eagle Bluff Lighthouse   58

     Pottawatomie Lighthouse on Rock Island 60

Contents

Plum Island Range Lights   63

Pilot Island Lighthouse   65

Cana Island Lighthouse   67

Old Baileys Harbor Lighthouse   71

Baileys Harbor Range Lights   72

Sturgeon Bay Ship Canal North Pierhead Light   76

Sturgeon Bay Ship Canal Lighthouse   78

Other Lake Michigan Lights   81

Algoma North Pierhead Light   82

Kewaunee Pierhead Lighthouse   84

Rawley Point Lighthouse   87

Two Rivers North Pierhead Light   88

Manitowoc North Breakwater Lighthouse   91

Sheboygan Breakwater Lighthouse   93

Old Port Washington Light Station   95

Port Washington Breakwater Light   97

Kevich Light   98

North Point Lighthouse   100

Milwaukee Breakwater Lighthouse   103

Milwaukee Pierhead Light   106

Wind Point Lighthouse   107

Racine Reef Lighthouse   110

Racine North Breakwater Light   112

Kenosha North Pierhead Light   114

Old Southport Lighthouse   116

Lighting The Way For The Future   119

Lighthouse Organizations and Restoration Efforts   123

Wisconsin Lighthouse Summary Table   125

About the Photography   126

Bibliography   127

Index   134

About the Authors   136

Acknowledgments

Having resided in Wisconsin all of our lives, we knew that the state was full of friendly people and abundant hospitality. We had no idea of the intense interest and the wealth of information and knowledge available concerning lighthouses. We feel we've only begun to scratch the historical surface on some of these lights. While criss-crossing the state photographing and researching information on Wisconsin's beacons, we met and corresponded with the nicest folks. So many people were helpful and willingly provided us with information and many interesting stories. Lighthouse enthusiasts are a unique and special breed of people. Without their collective help and cooperation, this lighthouse journey would have remained only an idea in the authors' minds and never would have been completed.

At the risk of omitting someone, we would like to thank:
Kay and George Sedivec who first introduced us to Cana Island twenty years ago and recently got us thinking about writing a book when innocently viewing our lighthouse photography, commenting, "you have such nice photos, you should write a book!"
Thomas Jones, U.S. Coast Guard Chief Warrant Officer, Milwaukee
Tom Dalske, Chief Boatswain's Mate, U.S. Coast Guard, Sturgeon Bay, WI
Vi Llewellyn, taxi driver extraordinaire, Washington Island
The Great Lakes Light Keepers Association (GLLKA), and especially Jean Gertz, the Lake Michigan Coordinator
Julie Zachau, Superior Public Library
Debbra Voss, Sheboygan Public Library
Mike Thomas, Neenah Public Library
The Algoma Public Library
Mary Ann Luplow, Sand Island, Volunteer Lightkeeper
John Bloomquist, water taxi driver, Apostle Islands Cruise Service
Judith A. Simonsen and Kevin Abing, Milwaukee County Historical Society
Timothy Harrison, Lighthouse Digest Magazine
Susan Rock, Ph.D., Rock Island History
David Nelson, 1st Mate of the Toscana
Captain Jean Bourne, R/V Pelagos
Mike Zimmer, Curator, Rogers Street Fishing Village and Museum, Two Rivers
Joel and Mary Blahnik, Chambers Island caretakers
Hickey Brothers of Baileys Harbor, for the use of their rowboat *Lars* (it leaked!!)
Sandy Zipperer and Mary Chris Naze of the Wisconsin Maritime Museum in Manitowoc
Thomas Schuller, Curator, Kewaunee County Historical Society
Mary Ann Platts, who also gave some great advice a few years back about photography: shoot what you love
Donald and Carol Henning
Al Krescanko, Racine
The unknown clerk at Orthober's in Sturgeon Bay who gave us directions to Sturgeon Bay Canal Park
Carol Boettcher, Ozaukee County Historical Society
Linda Nenn, Port Washington Historical Society
Jack A. Eckert, U.S. Coast Guard (retired)
The unknown owners of the Old Baileys Harbor Lighthouse who were gracious enough to allow us to photograph their light up close
The crew of the *Snowbird*, Ashland
Mike Borths, Fish Tales Guide Service, Menominee, Michigan
Mary Jane Herber, Brown County library
Bill Wangemann, Sheboygan Historian
Wayne Lemburg, Door County Historical Society, Eagle Bluff Light
Bob Gantner, Port Washington
Tom Bahti, WDNR

George Schemel, Racine
Nancy Emery, Door County Library, Sturgeon Bay
The Milwaukee Public Library, especially Liz Bender of the Frank P. Zeidler Humanities Room
Eileen Hannot Tork, Menominee County Historical Society
And Sue, Gary, and Nikki Zikmund for their moral support and encouragement

Special thanks to those who went above and beyond our requests to help us make this project a reality:
Bob Mackreth, Park Historian, Apostle Islands National Lakeshore
Edward C. Werner, Historian, Kenosha (Southport) Light Station
Eugene "Gene" Wilkins, Michigan Island, Volunteer Lightkeeper
Robert Couvillion, President, Peshtigo Historical Society
Thomas Pleger, Ph.D., Green Island Light Station
Lightkeepers, Kevich Light
Tim Sweet, Friends of Rock Island
Merle Baenen for his kindness and the wonderful guided tour of Green Bay on his yacht, Toscana
Dale Dempsey, U.S. Coast Guard, Aids to Navigation Team, Green Bay
Steven Karges, Ph.D., Lighthouse Historian
Francis and Doris Cornell for their historic photographs of Frank Drew and Green Island Light
    Station, the wonderful lunch and good conversation
Rick Bernstein and the State Historical Society of Wisconsin
Caroline Beckett and Frank Sandner, Flying Fish Graphics
Jerry Minnich, our editor and publisher at Prairie Oak Press, for his guidance and patience with a
    couple of rookie authors

viii

And last, but never least, to the best thing ever to happen to me, my partner, companion and wife Barb, whose gentle persistence allowed this dream to come true. I am so blessed. I love you, sweetie.

Definitely not last, my husband Ken, my "partner in lighthouses", my best friend and soul mate. Always asking "aren't you going to work on the book tonight?" in order to keep me going. You're the greatest!! I love you.

Heartfelt thanks to one and all. We had a ball!

—*Ken and Barb Wardius*

Note to the Reader

While searching through volumes of lighthouse data from many reputable sources, we encountered many inconsistencies. Most notable were the dates of construction and the heights of the towers.

Some of the differences exist because of a lack of uniformity, i.e. the year the light was authorized vs. when it was completed vs. when it was first lighted, etc. Tower heights also varied. Some heights were obviously focal planes (the vertical distance from the focal point of the lens to the water surface) and not the height of the tower. We tried to compromise when information from several credible references was found.

Not every single Wisconsin light is covered here. The most historically significant lights are showcased. We concentrated our efforts mostly on traditional lighthouses and excluded most lights that were metal light towers more than traditional lighthouses. Consequently, a number of lights, including the Pipe light tower on Lake Winnebago, Boyer Bluff light tower on Washington Island, Detroit Harbor Entrance Light at Washington Island, and Racine South Breakwater light are not featured. A few decorative lighthouses, as well as several private beacons not operated by the Coast Guard, are, however, highlighted.

For many lighthouses, there was a wealth of material available. For some beacons, however, there was little information. It is a shame that their stories will go untold for now.

We took great pains to insure the accuracy of this document. Please accept our apologies for any errors or omissions. Feel free to contact us with any updated information.

Ken and Barb Wardius
2240 West Marne Avenue
Glendale, Wisconsin 53209
Tel. 414-228-8947
E-mail: slw81@execpc.com

Wisconsin's Lighthouses

Lake Superior

Devils Island
Sand Island
Outer Island
Raspberry Island
Michigan Island Old Lighthouse
Michigan Island Light Tower
Chequamegon Point
La Pointe Light
Superior Breakwater
Ashland Breakwater

Apostle Islands Volunteer Lightkeeper

Pottawatomie Light
Plum Island
Chambers Island
Pilot Island
Eagle Bluff
Cana Island
Menominee Light
Old Baileys Harbor Light
Peshtigo Reef
Baileys Range Light
Sturgeon Bay Canal Light
Sherwood Point
Green Island
Sturgeon Bay Canal North Pierhead
Grassy Island Upper
Grassy Island Lower
Long Tail Point
Green Bay Entrance
Algoma Pierhead
Kewaunee Pierhead

Rawley Point

Neenah Lighthouse
Asylum Bay Lighthouse
Two Rivers Light
Rockwell Lighthouse
Lake Winnebago
Manitowoc Breakwater

Fond du Lac Light
Sheboygan Breakwater

Lake Michigan

Port Washington Breakwater & Old Port Washington Light
Kevich Light
North Point
Milwaukee Pierhead
Milwaukee Breakwater
Wind Point
Racine Breakwater Light
Kenosha Pierhead
Kenosha (Southport) Light

Map courtesy State Historical Society of Wisconsin

L

ighthouses. No symbol is more closely associated with the rich maritime tradition in Wisconsin, as well as the world, than the lighthouse. These historic beacons evoke a myriad of images: a bygone era, romance, loneliness, dependability, dedicated keepers manning the lights, eerie tales of haunted structures, and ghosts of past keepers. If these sentinels could talk, imagine the tales they could tell of ferocious storms taking their toll on vessels and people. Picture mariners of yesteryear, straining to see these beacons, anxiously hoping to make safe haven around rocky shorelines. A lighthouse, however, is much more than just a monument to keep ships from shoals, reefs, islands, and other obstacles. Each light has come to be a symbol of security and safety, a friend in a storm, if you will. These lights are synonymous with heroism, loyalty, danger, duty, and people caring for people. Sailors know the lights as welcoming beacons calling them home. History documents many a sailor peering through the darkness, searching for a light to greet him, depending upon these beacons to guide the weary mariner to safe harbor. Lighthouses are a reflection of the human spirit and a mirror to our past.

The world's oldest permanent man-made lighthouse dates to the third century BC when Alexander the Great was king of Macedonia. Sostratos, a Greek architect, designed the Pharos of Alexandria in Egypt. It was considered one of the original Seven Wonders of the Ancient World. Standing more than four hundred feet tall and shaped like a pyramid, it claimed the title of the tallest of all known lighthouses. Located on an island at the entrance to the Alexandria harbor, at dusk keepers lit a brilliant fire, backed by a large mirror, at the top of this gigantic tower. The Pharos served seagoing people for more than 1,500 years before an earthquake toppled it. So important was this ancient light, the word lighthouse is derived from pharos in several languages.

During the time of the Roman Empire at least thirty lighthouses were built along shores from the Black Sea to the Atlantic Ocean. Little factual information is known about some of these lights. Open wood fires probably fueled many of them.

The oldest active lighthouse on the planet is the

Milwaukee Pierhead Light at dawn

Roman-built light at La Coruna. Also known as the Tower of Hercules, this beacon was located near the border of today's Portugal, along the northwest coast of Spain. It dates to the fourth century AD. Two other European lighthouses were also built on the cliffs of Boulogne, France, and Dover, England. The Romans chose these sites because of their high cliffs. The lighthouses were only eighty feet tall, but stood almost four hundred feet above the level of the sea.

In 1696 a lighthouse at Eddystone in the English Channel was built over three years' time near the port of Plymouth. Eddystone was considered to be the most hazardous of reefs because wind and waves constantly bombarded the rocky shores. The first lantern room was installed here. Henry Winstanley, the builder of the original Eddystone light, had hoped to be in the lighthouse during "the greatest storm that ever was." On November 26, 1703, after the lighthouse had been in service for five years, its light was shining at midnight just as a great storm began to rage. Trees were uprooted and homes demolished. By morning the lighthouse was gone. All that remained were the broken metal rods used to secure it to the rocks. History records that Mr. Winstanley got his wish. He perished in his lighthouse during this notable tempest.

America is a leader in the number of lighthouses. It has been said that lighthouses are to America what castles are to Europe. In truth, United States lighthouses have been called "America's castles." No other country in the world has so elaborate a lighthouse system. The first lighthouse established in North America was at Boston in the autumn of 1716, in the colony of Massachusetts on Little Brewster Island. Whale oil was used as fuel. A cannon served as the first fog warning device here. During the American Revolution, the British damaged this structure extensively, making rebuilding it a necessity. The Boston Harbor Lighthouse also had the distinction of being the lone remaining light in the United States that had a keeper's presence. A special act of Congress in 1989 stipulated that this light continue to be permanently manned to preserve its historic reputation. Recently it was decided that even this keeper be eliminated. Plans call for the final lightkeeper, Coast Guardsman Richard Himelrick, to leave Boston Lighthouse when the National Park Service assumes responsibility for it. Other notable United States lights include the oldest, still standing, operational beacon at Sandy Hook, New Jersey, built in 1764. The tallest U.S. light is at Cape Hatteras, North Carolina, which towers 191 feet above the Atlantic Ocean. In 1999 it survived a move further inland to protect it from an eroding shoreline.

The year 1818 saw the first lighthouse on the Great Lakes at Fort Niagara, New York. By the middle 1800s more than two hundred lighthouses dotted these interior lakes. Eventually, twice that number served to protect ships on the Great Lakes, one of the highest concentrations of beacons anywhere in the world. In some Great Lakes areas there are few distinguishing landmarks and many of the lights were necessary to serve as pathfinders for mariners. Harbor entrances and dangerous passageways, reefs, shoals etc also needed to be lit.

Lighthouse Terminology

Catwalk—an elevated narrow walkway constructed of wood or metal raised above a pier or breakwater to allow safer access to a light in inclement weather.

Daymarker—the daytime markings on a lighthouse or other aid to navigation. Historical lights were daymarked by the shape and/or color of the tower. Modern lights use color coded patterns.

Rangelight with daymarker

Eclipse—an interval of darkness between appearances of a light; frequently used when there are multiple unequal periods of light and dark emitted from a beacon.

Fixed light—a light showing continuously and steadily.

Flashing light—a beacon which gives a short burst short of light.

Focal length—the distance of the focus from the surface of a lens.

Focal plane—the vertical distance from the focal point of the lens to the water surface.

Fog horn, fog signal—a horn sounded in foggy conditions to give warning.

GPS-global positioning system—a satellite-based radio navigation system with worldwide coverage providing navigation and position.

Iso (Isophase) light—a rhythmic light with equal light and dark periods.

Lantern room—the area in a lighthouse where the lantern and lens are housed.

Lens—a device for focusing or directing rays of light.

Nautical mile (nm)—also known as a sea mile, equal to approximately 6,078 feet. One nautical mile is equal to approximately 1.15 statute miles.

Occulting light—a light whose total duration of light is longer than the total duration of darkness and the intervals of darkness are of equal duration.

Parapet—a low wall or railing outside the lantern room platform used as a guardrail; also known as the gallery or the "widow's walk."

Range lights—a system involving two lights, one normally taller than the other, with one aligned in front of the other, that allows the mariner to arrange them vertically one over the other and is known as getting "on range." While on the water, the sailor can safely follow a straight-line course into a harbor or through a dangerous channel.

Parapet or "widow's walk"

Ventilator ball—The ball-shaped exterior top of the lantern room, which has many small holes that enabled the combustibles to be released from the burning fuel inside.

Winter light—A battery-powered beacon located outside the regular lantern room, used during off shipping season.

The Lighthouse

light'house, *n. tower with a navigational beacon. (Webster's)*

Far too simple a definition, stripped to its essential elements, the basic components of a lighthouse include a tower, watch, and lantern rooms, and usually a dwelling of some sort, either attached or nearby. A ventilator ball would top the light. Other miscellaneous structures such as fuel storage houses, an outhouse (privy was the typical name), a fog signal, or a boathouse might also be part of the lighthouse keeper's complex.

Some of the earliest lighthouses were built of stone or wood and were quite simple. One of the major difficulties related to wood was its susceptibility to fire. Stone towers could be built with locally available rock. Stones were placed one atop the other and cemented together with grout. These rocky monuments had to be massive at their foundations to support the immense weight of the tower.

In the 1800s different lighthouse styles began to emerge. The most widely used design included the keeper's home with the lantern constructed either on the roof or in a tower, which was part of the dwelling. Another style, the pier light, generally was smaller, more compact, and lighter than the standard tower and lightkeeper's quarters. Pier lights were designed simply and were built inexpensively. Keepers' quarters for these lights were typically on shore. Pierhead lights were common from the mid-1800s onward when many harbors were dredged and breakwaters and piers were constructed. Later in the century, when more lofty lights became necessary, cone-shaped brick towers were built. These structures were connected to the living quarters by a small walled passageway. Beginning around the 1860s, freestanding steel skeletal beacons were constructed. This design lessened the stress on an attached building during high winds and storms.

courtesy Port Washington Historical Society

Port Washington 1889 pierhead light and fishing tug

xiv

The Light

The light is the heart of the lighthouse. Since the first signal fire in ancient Egypt, the ritual of lighting the lamp has taken place every evening on waterways around the world. Many different materials have been used as fuels, including wood, coal, candles, and oils such as sperm whale, fish, colza (also known as cabbage or rapeseed), lard, and kerosene. The first light produced using wood or coal was not very bright. Crucial improvements occurred in the 1700s with the evolution of more effective oil-burning lamps that combined silver mirrors to magnify the light source. Of the various oils used, the most common included whale, lard, and kerosene. Sperm whale oil was preferred because it remained fluid in cold weather and was used through the 1840s. Sperm oil prices quadrupled by the 1860s as the whale population declined, necessitating a change to a more economical oil. Kerosene (mineral oil) became available in 1846 and was not only cheaper than whale oil but also burned more brilliantly. Originally kerosene was thought to be quite dangerous but its use became widespread by the late 1870s. The kerosene used in lighthouses was a special blend. It emitted a clear, white light, as opposed to previous fuels that produced a smoky, yellow flame.

The burning of coal and oils polluted the air and covered the interior glass of the lantern room with soot. This problem was reduced and finally eliminated with the use of "cleaner" fuels including natural gas, acetylene, and ultimately electricity.

Lamps were employed to hold and burn fuel. One of the earliest lighting systems was the Argand lamp, which produced a relatively bright light equal to seven candles. This lamp contained a round, hollow wick. Air was allowed to travel both outside and inside the wick, increasing the brightness of the flame while reducing smoke and fumes. Lamps used one to five wicks at the center. The larger the apparatus, the more numerous the wicks. Crude reflectors came into use and were soon improved upon. In the early 1800s Captain Winslow Lewis expanded upon the Argand lamp, adding a silver reflector, giving the setup a curved parabolic shape. Typically, sperm oil was the fuel used in Winslow Lewis lamps. The combination lamp and reflector produced a more brilliant light than the lamp alone. This system was relatively effective and inexpensive but soon became drastically inferior in light quality to a new shining star on the horizon, the Fresnel lens.

Augustin Jean Fresnel, (pronounced fra-nell'), a French physicist, born in the late eighteenth century, is credited with designing a lens that revolutionized lighthouses. Not recognized for his achievements during his lifetime, Fresnel, in 1822, developed the compound lens that would bear his name. The Fresnel lens design brought a marked improvement in the effectiveness of lighthouses, and the principle is still used in lens design today. Fresnel lenses were built with multiple tiers of prisms around the top and bottom that gathered all the light, produced parallel rays, and focused them into an extremely efficient, intense beam

Wind Point third-order Fresnel Lens

many times more powerful than anything before it. A shiny brass framework held the crystalline lens together. The shape of these hand-polished cut-glass lenses has been likened to a potbellied stove, a beehive, or a barrel. A fixed, steady light beam was produced unless the lens contained a center bulls-eye or a "flash" panel. A clockwork rotational mechanism revolved the lens at an exact speed and a flashing light was emitted. Often the mechanism controlled by the clock device had to be turned by hand every three to four hours. In this case, the trusty keeper never got an uninterrupted night's sleep! No mechanical clockwork equipment for lens turning survive. If a lens flashes today, it is rotated by an electric motor.

Three French companies built Fresnel lenses during that time. They included Barbier & Fenestre, Henri Le Paute, and Sautter, Lemonier & Cie, all of Paris. The lenses would be built in France, ferried unassembled across the ocean, and then erected in the lantern room of the lighthouse. The workmanship of these lenses is remarkable even by today's standards.

If an area possessed several lights, they would be distinguished from each other by color or by rhythms known as the light "characteristic" such as the length of flashing and the interval of time between flashes. This was the lights' signature. Sailors often referred to the flashing lights as those that "winked" at you in the darkness.

There are six sizes or "orders" of Fresnel lenses. The numbers signify different focal lengths. The range and concentration of the light produced varied accordingly. The first three orders are the largest, have the longest range, and are used for coastline lights. A first-order lens could be as tall as twelve feet and weigh three tons. Costs could approach $10,000. The smaller orders, four through six, were generally for harbor lights because they had shorter ranges. A sixth-order lens would stand only a foot and a half tall and cost significantly less. The most common Fresnel lenses on the Great Lakes were fourth-, fifth- and sixth-orders. An in-between size, the three-and-a-half-order lens, was also commonly used on the Great Lakes.

While preliminary expenses for Fresnel lenses were high, the magnification and concentration of the light beam decreased fuel costs to a quarter of what they had been previously. The strength of the light beam expanded nearly four to five times and increased the light's range twofold! Positioned a hundred feet above lake level, a Fresnel lens light could be seen as far as eighteen miles away. The first Fresnel lens in America was placed in 1841. By the end of the 1850s almost all U.S. lighthouses were using the French technology. Fresnel, the genius who has been termed the "father of the modern lighthouse" for his invention, died at age thirty-nine.

Today, the fundamentals of the Fresnel lens can be seen in many places. A few of the modern uses of the Fresnel system include car headlights, traffic signals, the flashing lights of emergency vehicles, and movie projector lights. The "fish eye" mirror utilized by truck drivers and the plastic "lens" mounted on the rear window of motor homes to enhance the field of rear vision use optic principles from Monsieur Fresnel.

By the 1930s most of the lights using the Fresnel lens with oil and wick lamps had been replaced by incandescent lights which increased the strength of the beam even further, from tens of thousands of candlepower to as many as several million.

Another lamp first used around 1910 was the incandescent oil vapor lamp. Much like the Coleman lantern of today, a mantle was employed and the fuel was vaporized. A significantly brighter light was produced. Incandescent electric lamps would later become the norm.

Different types of lantern rooms existed. The uncommon "birdcage" style, which from a distance indeed resembled a birdcage, was found around the mid-1800s. The eight- to ten-sided lantern room we see today, however, was the most prevalent. Slowly, standard styles of lighthouses emerged on the Great Lakes, leading to many similar lights being constructed. Standard design criteria for lighthouse building were promoted during this era. Approximately six different reliable designs were recommended and repeatedly used. Because of this, some lights on the Great Lakes are virtual copies of one another. This duplication in design resulted in both efficiency and cost-savings in the building of lighthouses. Today, Wisconsin has several lights that look similar to each other. For example, Sand Island, Chambers Island, and Eagle Bluff lighthouses share a similar style. Green Island, Pottawatomie, and Old Port Washington lights also share design characteristics.

Many lighthouses were also frequently equipped with another lifesaving apparatus, the fog signal. If conditions were poor for light visibility, mariners as well as landlubbers could hear the horns' mournful sound. If a sailor could not establish his position because the light was obstructed, he could rely on the periodic blasts of the howling foghorn. Fog devices varied throughout the years. In the early 1850s mechanical fog bells and air fog whistles were used. Later, steam-powered fog whistles gave way to fog sirens. The majority of fog signals in service on the Great Lakes in the early 1900s were steam train whistles. The chief problem with this type of fog signal was the time it took to become fully operational—

nearly an hour. In that time, a ship could get into serious trouble or the fog could vanish. Gasoline-powered fog engines soon followed. In the 1930s fog signals were converted to electricity and could be powered up by remote control. No original nineteenth-century steam-driven fog signals are in use today.

The dawn of electric light in the late 1800s was an exciting development in the efficiency of lighthouses. Electricity was first employed at a U.S. lighthouse in 1886 to light the Statue of Liberty. It took several decades, however, for electricity to become widespread in U.S. lights. Other advances included timers that automatically turned the lamps on and off, and a rotating mechanism to self-replace a burned out electric bulb. Soon after the arrival of electricity at more light stations in the 1920s, automation of the lights and fog signals followed. By the middle of the twentieth century almost all Great Lakes lighthouses were electrically powered.

The Keeper

While the light was the heart of the lighthouse, the keeper was truly its soul. Many keepers and their families devoted an appreciable portion of their lives to these beacons. They toiled many hours of the day and night, keeping vigil over their precious lights. During the earliest days when boats plied the waters of Wisconsin and around the globe, the central goal of the lightkeeper has always been to keep the lamp lit. At times keepers fought to keep the flame burning and endured periods of isolation, loneliness, monotony, harsh weather conditions, and arduous living conditions. In some precarious locations, the keepers and their lighthouses were exposed to severe storms. With nowhere else to go, the keeper rode out each tempest in the lighthouse. Everyday necessities we take for granted today did not exist. There was no indoor plumbing. At many freshwater stations water was carried from the nearby body of water. If the weather was raging, water was hard to obtain or it was of poor quality. Wood-burning stoves were necessary in heating the dwelling and cooking meals.

These pioneers were stalwarts. In many ways they were just ordinary people who at times were faced with very extraordinary circumstances. The keepers were mostly average folks, typically hardworking, and thankful for a steady job with regular income. Lighthouse people were a hardy lot and for the most part took pride in discharging their duties. The light stations and surrounding grounds were reflections of the keepers and their families. Not a job for the faint of heart, light keeping was a way of life and certainly no cakewalk. Today we tend to over-romanticize lighthouse life. Most times it was not glamorous. Put yourself in the shoes of the keeper, climbing tall towers or walking out to pier lights with buckets of fuel, winding mechanisms for flashing beacons every few hours, cleaning and polishing glass and brass endlessly, keeping the lighthouse grounds ship-shape, etc. The list seems endless.

The position of lightkeeper was highly prized and considered prestigious. Many of the earliest keepers were hand-picked. Some were dependent upon political assignment. Patronage at times won out over a keeper's

Chambers Island spiral stairway

xviii

courtesy Francis and Doris Cornell

Frank Drew, Green Island lightkeeper

faithful service. Because the government was intimately involved with lighthouses, their connection to history and politics is obvious. There are many examples of multiple family members joining the Lighthouse Service, including fathers and sons, brothers and uncles. It was common to see records involving several generations of the same family, oftentimes serving the same lighthouse.

Once the Lighthouse Board came into being, much was done to bring these jobs under an entitlement system. In the early 1850s the Lighthouse Board found the competency of keepers to vary widely, and it was recommended that keepers test for the position. There are numerous records of keepers performing less than adequately.

A lightkeeper candidate had to be at least eighteen years of age, be literate (in the earliest days, many keepers were not), be fit to do manual labor, and have some mechanical and sailing aptitude. The board did as much as possible to control political appointments of keepers. Lighthouse keepers were included under the Civil Service system in 1896. The board continued to advocate lighthouse keepers as a professional service. Numerous people advanced in the Lighthouse Service, from secondary positions such as assistants to that of keeper. The Lighthouse Board also instituted a uniform for male lightkeepers, consisting of a dress uniform as well as fatigues for working. The dress uniform incorporated a coat, trousers, vest, and cap, all made of dark blue flannel or jersey. Two rows of five yellow metal buttons dressed up the front of the double-breasted coat. The cloth cap had a lighthouse badge fastened immediately above the bill.

Salaries of keepers were paltry. In the early 1800s the pay was $200 to $250 per year. By the 1840s the pay was approximately $400 per year. In the mid-1850s Congress legislated the average annual pay to be $600 and this wage remained steady for decades. The keeper and his family, however, were provided a house and supplies and most light station grounds had room for a vegetable garden and some fruit trees. Some keepers kept chickens and cows. For many years there was no retirement plan. But in 1918 Congress passed an act that allowed retirement at age sixty-five with thirty years of service.

xix

M*any keepers devoted most of their adult lives to lighthouses. Joseph Napiezinski, a lightkeeper at Rawley Point and other Wisconsin lights, served the Lighthouse Service for forty-eight years!*

The Keeper's Tasks

By regulation, the light had to be ignited thirty minutes before sunset, kept burning all night, and extinguished thirty minutes after dawn every day. There was little room for excuses when it came to having a dependable working light. The keepers were in charge of insuring that the light remained lit by keeping the fuel replenished and repeatedly, every few hours or so, pruning the wicks precisely to insure a clean burn. This chore gave rise to them being known as "wickies." Keepers needed to monitor oil consumption precisely, as well.

Many of the keeper's duties were learned on the job. If a keeper was fortunate enough to have an assistant, each worked a twelve-hour watch, noon to midnight and midnight to noon. At night with the light burning it was the keeper's duty to make sure, if his light had a cyclic signal, that its timing remained uniform. The machinery that turned the light had to be wound every three to four hours. This was accomplished by calibrating weights of more than a hundred pounds.

The keepers had to clean and polish the lens often, in many cases several times daily. Soot and smoke built up on the lens to obscure the light. It was also imperative that the chimney of the lens room be kept open and spotless. Smoke in the lens room would affect the clarity of the light and could cause the light to be dimmed. If a fog signal was part of the light station, it had to be kept in working condition.

Another important duty was the keeping of the daily log. Most days it was simply a weather report or a mention of ships passing in the distance. On occasion when there were visitors to the lighthouse, this was also noted.

A formal publication of the Treasury Department, "Instructions to Light-Keepers" (circa. 1902) was printed for employees who tended the lights. Some of the basic keeper's rules included:

Eagle Bluff oil lamp, book and keeper's glasses

Should a keeper be delinquent in his or her duties, the assistant keeper is to notify the inspector immediately. Failure to maintain a burning light is grounds for dismissal.

Keepers must be familiar with all equipment in their care.

Keepers must be considerate of all visitors.

Keepers may not charge admission to those visiting the lighthouse.

Drunken persons will not be allowed to remain at the station and drunken keepers will be dismissed from duty.

Keepers are expected to make repairs to the station. Should workers be employed to make repairs, the keepers are required to aid them.

Total and complete neatness of the buildings and property is expected.

Keepers must report to the inspector any shipwrecks that occur in proximity of their respective stations.

Keepers must maintain a daily journal, recording the operations of the lighthouse.

When lights became powered by electricity, the problem of soot obscuring the lenses was eliminated. Now the keepers need not spend so much time maintaining the light. However, this did not mean the keepers had newfound spare time. The lenses were inspected for chips or cracks, kept free of dust, and light bulbs needed changing. Interior and exterior painting or polishing of brass was done frequently. U.S. Lighthouse Service and later Coast Guard regulations insisted that the whole location be flawlessly cared for. This was ongoing duty since nature had a way of insuring plenty of work. Slowly, with the advent of electricity, however, many lighthouses no longer needed personnel to tend the beacons routinely. Eventually millions of dollars would be saved by automating the lights.

Another advance, radio communication, also allowed the keepers to speak with the ships that relied on them. The manned lighthouse was slowly becoming a thing of the past. Modern improvements in radar and radio beacons, along with today's satellite technology and Global Positioning Systems (GPS) have rendered the lighthouse to a less important status. Clearly the need for lighthouses has been significantly reduced. The U.S. Coast Guard finalized automation of all United States lighthouses, except the Boston Harbor Lighthouse, in 1992. The need for mortal keepers had been eliminated.

Women Keepers

Although predominantly a white, male organization, the U.S. Lighthouse Service was not an exclusive men's club. There were an impressive number of women chief keepers and even more women who served as assistant keepers. Normally, the wife of the keeper became the assistant keeper. If the husband died, his wife was his logical replacement. The first women governmental employees were most likely lighthouse keepers. This phenomenon was not because the Lighthouse Service was ahead of its time in the equal employment of women. It was simply a way of keeping costs down. Many keepers were married and it was economical to have a husband and wife pair on the payroll rather than pay for two individual living quarters.

Lighthouse keeping was definitely a family affair. Women played significant roles both directly and indirectly in the bountiful history of many U.S. and Wisconsin lighthouses. They learned the workings of the lights and tended them as well as their male counterparts. Many tales of women rescuing sailors can also be found. In addition, the everyday care of the family was the women's responsibility. Without a doubt, the women were true lighthouse heroines. Their contributions were impressive.

Several Wisconsin lighthouses, including beacons in the Apostle Islands, Sherwood Point, the Kenosha (Southport) Light, and the Old Port Washington Light Station, had a significant woman's presence. Some of the women performed lighthouse duties into their seventies.

As with families of the time, children who grew up in lighthouses walked to school. When harsh Wisconsin winters created high snowdrifts, tunnels were dug so the children could find their way to school. For children who lived at island lights, a daily boat trip back and forth to the mainland was normal. In remote locations, a parent, usually the mother, took on the role of educator as well. Schooling could also take place after the navigation season was completed with island-dwelling families moving to the mainland each winter.

United States Lighthouse Agencies

One of the initial acts and priorities of our fledgling country's first Congress dealt with lighthouses. In 1789 it was determined that the Treasury Department would be responsible for the building and maintenance of light stations by passing the National Lighthouse Act. The federal government controlled the lights and dictated rules to the states. Alexander Hamilton was the first commander of U.S. lighthouses. Early in our country's history, the president played an active and direct role in decisions regarding lighthouses, including the hiring and firing of keepers. Many of the earliest lights in the

United States were the first public works projects. Growing trade in various eastern coastal areas of the country necessitated additional lights. Originally financial support for aids to navigation came from fees levied on ships entering U.S. ports. Beginning in 1801, Congress funded lighthouses.

Succeeding Hamilton as lighthouse commandant was Stephen Pleasonton. An able administrator, bureaucrat, and bookkeeper, with no engineering or maritime background, Pleasonton ruled like a dictator for several decades (1820-1852). Officially titled the 5th Auditor of the Treasury Department, and the Superintendent General of Lighthouses, Pleasonton oversaw the construction of hundreds of new beacons. His miserly ways, however, contributed to the decline in the condition of many lights. Pleasonton supported the Winslow Lewis lamp and prohibited the use of the technologically superior Fresnel lens for many years. He was alone responsible for the delay in instituting the Fresnel lens system in the United States. Numerous decisions regarding lighthouses during this period were politically motivated and some bordered on or were obviously corrupt.

Many complaints, especially from mariners, arose that the lighthouse system in the United States needed revamping. By the middle of the 1800s a diverse group of people advocated conversion to the Fresnel lens in this country. Superintendent Pleasonton continued to delay the implementation of this vastly superior lens, insisting that tests and more information were needed. A Lighthouse Board consisting of the Secretary of the Treasury, military officers, scientists, engineers, and government secretaries, among others, was formed in 1852 and continued for more than half a century. That same year, Pleasonton was finally removed from office. Lighthouse districts were formed. Expeditious enhancements were made to light stations. The performance of many lighthouses and keepers improved during this period. Detailed written instructions of duties were furnished to all lightkeepers. Additionally, the Fresnel lens was touted as the light of choice. The Lighthouse Board was a strong advocate and the lens's use became far-reaching. By the time of the Civil War, Fresnel lenses were in use in lighthouses all over America. Mariners described the light from these lenses as blazing compared to the antiquated lamps and reflectors they replaced.

Beginning in 1910 the Lighthouse Board evolved into the Bureau of Lighthouses, which also became known as the Lighthouse Service. The progressive leadership of George R. Putnam, the first Commissioner of Lighthouses, directed by the Secretary of Commerce, shaped the agency in a positive manner for decades. The slow process of becoming more of a civilian agency and less of a military one unfolded. A prevailing statement used by the Lighthouse Service during these times of change was "In the interest of economy and efficiency in administration . . ." Advancements in radio technology, particularly the radio beacon, a retirement system, and other improvements marched forward. By the 1920s telephones also became more commonplace. At the height of its reign in 1940, the Lighthouse Service employed more than five thousand people.

From its beginnings, the Lighthouse Service discriminated against African Americans. No proof has been found that any black man ever served as a lighthouse keeper. Blacks were specifically excluded from the Lighthouse Service except to serve as cooks on lightships.

In July, 1939, President Franklin Roosevelt and the Congress, because of the threat of war overseas, discontinued the Lighthouse Service. Administration of aids to navigation was transferred back to the military, specifically the United States Coast Guard (USCG). The decades of the 1940s and 1950s saw the beginnings of many lights being automated while the 1960s witnessed nearly complete automation. Eventually the cost-effective measures of massive light automation took over the system. The Coast Guard's role would now primarily involve routine maintenance of the lights while a rare few on the Great Lakes would continue to be manned. The long technological voyage of the lighthouse in the United States, starting with whale-oil lamps and candles, gave way in many cases to fully automated, solar-powered electric lamps. Some would argue that the "depersonalization" of the lights was a necessity of progress. The light's only real purpose, they argued, was safety. Others would contend that the passing of the faithful lightkeeper and the outright abandonment of many lights was not an occasion to celebrate but one to mourn.

Lightships and Tenders

Mobile, floating lights—lightships—were placed at locations where it was difficult to erect a permanent beacon. Lightships were efficient aids to navigation during the day as well as night. Not an assignment for the person with a weak stomach, light vessels contended with many a stormy sea. Even experienced sailors would sometimes become seasick. Lightship duty could be both hazardous and lonely. The first lightship in the United States was placed in the Chesapeake Bay in 1820. The inaugural Great Lakes lightship was placed between Lakes Michigan and Huron in 1837. Dozens of lightships were on duty in the United States. At least two lightships guided mariners in Wisconsin. Originally constructed of wood, lightships eventually were made of iron or steel. These vessels oftentimes lacked propulsion of their own, and were towed to a site and anchored.

Within the Lighthouse Service was another group of vessels known as tenders. Their job was to convey personnel, much-needed supplies, and equipment, including food, fuel, paint, soap, visitors, and news, to many light stations. While keepers and their families looked forward to visits from the tenders and welcomed them with open arms, many times this also meant the coming of the Lighthouse Inspector. Arriving unannounced and capable of administering the "white glove test," the inspector commanded high respect. Lightkeepers and their families wanted to make a favorable impression. A poor report from the inspector could mean the possibility of removal from the position. However, the inspector's visit did have a positive side. He brought news of the outside world and, beginning in the mid-1870s, traveling libraries, as well. Approximately fifty books with subjects including poetry, science, history, novels, and religious volumes were circulated to lightkeepers to combat boredom, especially as it existed at remote locations. These library collections were generally issued twice a year.

For reasons unknown, starting in the middle 1860s, tenders were generally named after shrubs, trees, or flowers. For example, the *Marigold* frequented Lake Superior while the *Hyacinth* served many lighthouses on Lake Michigan. The *Sumac* and *Dahlia* were other tenders in these waters.

Special lifesaving stations also played a role in maritime safety. The beginnings of what would later become the U.S. Life-Saving Service was begun in the late 1700s. These structures were regularly positioned near lighthouses or harbor entrances to rescue people stranded close to shore after shipwrecks. In 1855 there were twenty-three lifesaving stations on Lake Michigan and one on Lake Superior. The stations typically were equipped with lifeboats and equipment to secure a lifeline to nearby vessels in distress. A surprising number of Wisconsin communities were home to these helpful aids, including Plum Island in Door County, Kewaunee, Milwaukee, Racine, and Kenosha, among others.

In the 1850s lightship crew members were paid twenty cents a day.

courtesy Milwaukee County Historical Society

Milwaukee Lightship

Lighthouse tender

The Great Lakes

Appropriately named, the Great Lakes are a significant part of our heritage. They are considered to be the "fourth seacoast" of the United States. Constituting approximately twenty per cent of the world's and ninety per cent of the United States' fresh water, they are the largest fresh, surface water source on our planet and the earth's most expansive interior watercourse. The Great Lakes are a thousand-mile water transportation connection from Superior-Duluth on the west to the St. Lawrence Seaway on the east. This thoroughfare has played a major role in the development and history of Wisconsin and of the country.

A critical link in the U.S. economy, the Great Lakes helped to fuel a growing nation. The waterways were the superhighways of yesteryear, vital to the economic development of the region as well as America as a whole. They connected raw materials and consumers. Moving goods and people nationwide via water transit was the most practical, least expensive, and most reliable method in the early history of our country. Early in our history, if materials were not moved via waterways, they had to be transported overland by wagon. Remember that the elaborate modern system of railways, roads, and interstate highways we enjoy today was not in place. But maritime success also exacted a costly toll in lives and ships lost. The increase in shipping, movement of goods, economic growth of the Great Lakes, and commerce in general necessitated the construction of more lighthouses as traffic in shipping lanes increased. Great Lakes lighthouses were an integral cog in the expansion of nautical trade from the middle of the nineteenth century through the early twentieth. America's maritime connection is directly associated with lighthouses.

The Great Lakes have been one of the most important transportation systems in the U.S. since the beginning of the 1800s. In the years following the Civil War, the Great Lakes teemed with vessels hauling wood, grain, and other products to expanding markets nationwide. By the end of the nineteenth century, ports saw thousands of arrivals and departures annually. Beginning with wooden schooners and later steel-hulled boats, today thousand-foot super carriers travel Great Lakes waters. The Great Lakes remain a transportation hub for America in contemporary times.

These titanic inland bodies of water, also known as "sweet water seas," historically brew storms that rival those of the world's oceans. Storms on the Great Lakes can be fierce and deadly. Approximately 3,500 ships have gone to their graves on the Great Lakes. November is typically the month filled with the most shipwrecks. A glance through historical

Freighter, Door County strait

records reveals a succession of tragic and immense gales. Dates and fatalities are numerous: November 11, 1835, "swept the lakes clear of sails." October 15, 1880, saw Lake Michigan and Door County battle the Alpena Gale. 1905 was another deadly year on the Great Lakes. The "great storm of 1913" killed more than 250 sailors and damaged or sank a dozen vessels. Many Wisconsinites still remember the lethal storm of November 11, 1940. More recently, in 1975, Lake Superior claimed a modern freighter, the *Edmund Fitzgerald*. When the Great Lakes have become gale-ravaged, lighthouses without a doubt have saved many lives. With the Great Lakes navigation season consuming much of the calendar year (normally open from approximately late March to early December) these tempests will continue to be a force to be reckoned with.

The people who built lighthouses at various Great Lakes locations confronted many obstacles in construction. Building engineers had to solve problems of towering bluffs, shoals, sandy beaches, and other obstacles. Construction crews were often confronted by high winds, rough seas, and dizzying heights in order to build "sea-worthy" beacons. The earliest lighthouse on the Great Lakes was built in 1818 near Buffalo, New York. The first Lake Michigan lighthouse was located at the mouth of the Chicago River in 1832. Quite a few of the first lights on Lake Michigan were built at the mouths of rivers, to serve adjacent communities.

Wisconsin

The state is named after the Wisconsin River, which diagonally bisects it. A French version of an Ojibwa term for the river translates to "gathering of the waters." The Badger State is also bordered on several sides by other significant waterways. Located at the headwaters of both the Great Lakes and Mississippi River systems, our state was an ideal location for attracting settlers and maritime trade became the backbone of local economies. Waterborne commerce was the lifeblood of Wisconsin.

In the first half of the 1800s approximately a third of a million people resided in what would become the state of Wisconsin. Agriculture, forestry, and fishing were the predominant occupations of the day. The primary products transported were wood, ore, grain and coal. Industrial development increased dramatically in the 1850s. Wisconsin was also a major shipbuilding center in the nineteenth century. Most major Wisconsin cities with a tributary stream connecting to the Great Lakes possessed a lighthouse. The growth of commerce and the increasing size of vessels on the Great Lakes led to the need for harbor development. Piers were built, harbors dredged, and aids to navigation installed. Most Wisconsin ports sported pierhead lights beginning roughly in the 1870s. Most of Wisconsin's lighthouses began their service between 1850 and 1900. Wisconsin's inaugural light, Pottawatomie, dates to 1836.

Wisconsin become a territory in 1836 and achieved statehood in 1848. For more than 160 years, the lights have assisted mariners through Lakes Superior, Winnebago, and Michigan. The lighthouses blazed a trail through the darkness, serving as nautical "night lights." Lighthouses have played a tremendous role in shaping Wisconsin into the diverse state it is today.

Wisconsin beacons have their own personalities and characteristics. Several of them are unique, being lone surviving representatives of certain types or styles of lighthouses. From the westernmost reaches of Lake Superior and the northern limits of the Apostle Islands, to inland Lake Winnebago, to the bay of Green Bay, to vacationland Door County and the entire length of the western shore of Lake Michigan, these beacons have innumerable tales to tell. Like people, each lighthouse is different. Let us attempt to capture the essence of each light with a photo and by recounting some of its history and lore.

Lake Superior.

Wisconsin's "north shore" begins with the mighty lake named Superior. Known to the Native American Chippewa as *Gitche Gumee*, Superior is the largest freshwater lake in the world. Covering more than 31,000 square miles, it is the deepest and coldest of the Great Lakes. This immense lake measures more than 350 miles in length and 150 miles in width, covering in excess of 2,700 miles of shoreline. The lake is an average of nearly 500 feet deep with a maximum depth of almost a quarter mile.

Probably "discovered" by the French explorer Etienne Brule, one of Samuel de Champlain's scouts, in the early 1620s, Superior's waved-washed beaches and shorelines contain half of all the water in the Great Lakes. More than an eighth of the earth's fresh water is contained here. The lake rarely freezes over, but ice along the shores closes ports from approximately December to April.

The western end of Lake Superior was settled later than most of the remainder of the Great Lakes region. Fur trading, lumbering, fishing, and mining promoted economic growth of the area.

Fleets of freighters have ventured across the massive blue waterway of Superior for decades, carrying bulk commerce to the world. Lake Superior is one the busiest shipping lakes on the globe. Iron ore and copper were two of the primary early commodities being transported to iron and steel mills to the east. Lighthouses first appeared here in the mid-1800s and will likely always be a part of Superior's story.

Pictured Rocks National Lakeshore

When unleashing her wrath, storm-angered Superior can be treacherous and downright hostile. Nearly five hundred ships have been engulfed by the lake's fury, adding credence to the Native American Ojibwa belief that cold Superior "never gives up her dead." Many a spouse of Lake Superior's sailors and lighthouse keepers grew to hate the lake because of her vengeance.

Today massive super carriers travel the waters of Lake Superior, their captains ever wary, even today, of the force of the lake and how many have lost their lives here.

Superior

Historically, the city of Superior has been a shipping port of great importance. Founded in 1853, Superior experienced rapid growth in the second half of the nineteenth century, when the volume of shipping through the neighboring waters increased dramatically. Iron ore and grain were two of the major commodities moved through this port.

Wisconsin Point Light (Superior Entry South Breakwater Light)

Jointly, Wisconsin Point and Minnesota Point stretch ten miles across the far southwestern tip of Lake Superior. Comprising the largest freshwater sandbar on the planet, sand deposits from the lake and rivers created this sandbar three thousand years ago. The natural opening to Superior Bay was dangerous in windy weather. The thin, shallow natural channel, first charted in 1861, separates Superior Bay, Allouez Bay and the open Lake. The first ore shipped from the Mesabi Iron Range near Duluth, Minnesota, passed through the entry in 1893. The original channel was only four to sixteen feet deep. The U.S. Corps of Engineers completed the modern-day channel that is five hundred feet wide and thirty-two feet deep. Today Superior is one of the busiest ports in the United States and manages shipments of coal, grain, and iron ore to destinations around the world. Wisconsin Point Light sits slightly more than two miles northeast from where the isthmus juts into the bay.

Built in 1913, this Douglas County lighthouse is unique in that its base is oval in shape, while the concrete light tower is round. The structure is supported by a foundation secured in the lake bottom. Positioned at the west pierhead entrance to Superior Harbor at the western end of Wisconsin Point, this beacon replaced a lighthouse on the easterly end of Minnesota Point that was built in 1854 and today stands alone in ruins. A ten-foot-high concrete pier serves to anchor this light at the end of a concrete and giant stone south breakwater. A fourth-order Fresnel lens originally emitted a white light. Two lighthouse keeper residences still stand nearby. The tower itself is forty-two feet tall, having a fifty-two foot focal plane. The building consists of eleven rooms and a full basement. Although the original fog signal equipment no longer survives, the light today still has a functional fog warning signal.

Originally the walkway to the lighthouse was a two-thousand-foot pier with a steel cable for the keepers to hold onto when waves washed over the pier. According to Keeper David Simonson, "When we have a northeaster, blue water pours over this pier. If we're walking on it, we hoist ourselves up by the cable when a wave comes, to avoid being washed off." Following a severe storm during the winter of 1967, the U.S. Corps of Engineers placed huge boulders along the breakwater for added protection. The enormous stones were blasted from the stony shores of Isle Royal and transported here. Today golden lichens cover the boulders.

On November 9, 1975, shortly before 2 p.m., the giant ore carrier Edmund Fitzgerald *slipped through the Superior breakwater on her way to a date with tragedy. Nearby, the Wisconsin Point Light blinked what would turn out to be a final goodbye. Less than thirty hours later, in heavy seas, during the worst storm seen on the Great Lakes in thirty years, the Fitzgerald sank fifteen miles from the shelter of Lake Superior's Whitefish Bay. Before taking twenty-nine men to a watery grave, "Big Fitz" battled gale-force winds clocked at eighty miles per hour and thirty-foot waves.*

Sunrise at Wisconsin Point Light

Current status: Active aid to navigation. Rotating green beacon flashes every five seconds, visible for 22 miles. Fog signal sounds a three-second blast in a thirty-second period.

How to get there: From the southeast take highway 2/53 to Moccasin Mike Road. Turn right (northeast) onto Moccasin Mike Rd. and go approx. 1.5 miles to a paved road that does not have a name (there is a sign just before this road that indicates the way to the lighthouse). Turn left (north) on this unmarked road. The road also passes the site of a former Chippewa Indian Burial Ground. Follow the road approximately 3.25 miles until it ends in parking lot to your right (east). Walking out to view the light up close is a tricky task. A good portion of the .25 mile trek involves navigating across boulders. Watch your step! Additionally, the fields surrounding the parking lot and sandy beach are littered with poison ivy.

Apostle Islands

"The trouble with our life here is that we have too much time to think"

—a lightkeeper reflecting on the loneliness and monotony at a Lake Superior Light Station.

The Apostle archipelago consists of twenty-two islands located in the western end of Lake Superior off the northeast coast of Bayfield and Ashland counties in the northernmost part of the Badger State. The islands are mere specs in this enormous section of Lake Superior. Two primary explanations about the islands' birth can be found. According to Native American lore, the isles were the result of a chase between a hunter and a deer. Unable to catch the animal, the unsuccessful hunter threw a handful of earth into the water in frustration, with the islands rising from these bits of soil. Another interpretation is geologic, the landmasses being formed by glaciers thousands of years ago.

Historically, this area was home to Native American Ojibwa. Although the exact time of their arrival is uncertain, estimates range from the 1400s to the late 1600s. French explorers and fur traders "discovered" and named the Apostle Islands in 1659. (The French commonly assigned religious names to geographic locations they visited.) Miners, missionaries, seamen, lumbermen, and fishermen were some of the early inhabitants. Timber, iron ore, and fish were important early components of the regional economy. In the nineteenth century, brownstone quarried from some of the Apostle Islands was another valuable commodity, used in buildings throughout the Midwest. Today the regional economy is fueled by tourism.

The birth of Apostle light stations paralleled the increased commercial development in the surrounding area, which included Bayfield, La Pointe, Ashland, and Superior-Duluth. A century of busy shipping justified the existence of the lighthouses. These lights were placed at strategic locations to be protective signposts for ships. When the canal at Sault Ste. Marie, Michigan (the "Soo" canal) was finished in 1855, it connected the western Great Lakes with eastern United States ports and, thereby, to ports of the world. The Soo Locks reduced shipping time and consequently costs. A century ago this was the busiest shipping channel in the country, and lighthouses were built to warn and protect the thousands of mariners and ships that traversed these waters. Lighthouses have been guiding mariners and ships in this region since the mid- to late 1800s. Many of these outposts at times were quite remote. It was normal for keepers to be deprived of news of the outside world for considerable periods. Despite their isolation, a camaraderie existed among many of the families stationed at the Apostle light stations and turnover of lighthouse personnel was low. Sudden climate changes also posed problems. Dangerous "lake effect" weather changes have always occurred quickly here, making this area of Lake Superior particularly hazardous for mariners. Approximately a hundred ships have been wrecked in this area.

The Apostle Islands National Lakeshore, one of only four designated National Lakeshores in the United States, was established in 1970. Its natural splendor is an absolute public treasure. Consisting of twenty-one islands dispersed over 69,000 acres, approximately sixty per cent of the Lakeshore lies above water. Madeline Island is not included as part of the National Lakeshore because it already had significant development. The Apostles boast the grandest assortment of lighthouses found in our National Parks. Here, you can visit an incomparable grouping of unique, historically significant light stations, which have been called "gems in a jeweled necklace." All of the Apostle Islands lights are listed on the National Register of Historic Places, and the structures are quite well preserved by the National Park Service. The majority of Apostles light stations continue their original function, guiding vessels around the islands. Placed in critical areas, stations on Sand, Devils, and Outer islands mark the outer perimeter of the Apostles. Raspberry, Michigan, and Long Island lighthouses mark interior Apostle Islands positions. The grounds are open to the public, but the buildings are closed unless park personnel, many of them volunteers, are present to provide guided tours. From June to September a park ranger is stationed on Raspberry Island and National Park Service volunteers live at Sand, Devils, Michigan, and Outer islands for two-week "tours of duty." Daily hours are usually from 9 a.m. until 4 p.m. The station on Long Island is not regularly staffed during the summer but can be viewed from the water.

An excellent place to begin a tour is at the Apostle Islands National Lakeshore Headquarters in Bayfield, located on Washington Ave. between 4th and 5th streets. This striking building, formerly the county courthouse, is made of brownstone quarried locally. You can start with an introductory video presentation about the islands and view a lighthouse display. The headquarters also houses the original three-and-a-half-order Fresnel lens that once illuminated the original Old Michigan Island Lighthouse. Contact the Apostle Islands National Lakeshore, Route 1, Box 4, Bayfield, WI 54814; phone

courtesy National Park Service

Devil's Island Volunteer Lightkeeper

(715) 779-3397. Their website is an outstanding interactive information and educational tool: www.nps.gov/apis/

Both the National Park Service and the U.S. Coast Guard care for the lighthouses of the Apostle Islands. The maintenance of buildings and grounds in the Apostles is under the direction of the National Park Service while the actual servicing of the lights is the responsibility of the U.S. Coast Guard.

All of the Apostle Island lighthouses can be reached by boat. Contact the Apostle Islands Cruise Service, P.O. Box 691, Bayfield City Dock, Bayfield WI 54814. Phone (715) 779-3925 or (800) 323-7619. Also visit them on line at www.apostleisland.com. Several boats, including the Island Princess, feature daily cruises to various lights seasonally. Special lighthouse cruises as well as individual water taxi services are available. An Annual Apostle Islands Lighthouse Celebration is also held in September. It features special narrated lighthouse tours, boat cruises to all the lights, displays, and lectures by National Park Service staff. The celebration is a must for the lighthouse enthusiast.

Sand Island Lighthouse

Sand Island is located the most westward of any of the major Apostle Islands. An increase in Lake Superior shipping necessitated a light here. For upbound ships it points the way to Superior-Duluth. Sailors were concerned about the absence of lights between Raspberry Island to the east and the city of Superior to the west. A western light outpost was needed. Built in 1881 with locally quarried Apostle Island brownstone, the light rests on the north end of the island, immediately north and east of Lighthouse Bay. The lighthouse has a forty-four-foot tower and attached two story keepers quarters. Sand Island Light's architectural style, Norman Gothic, is identical to several other Wisconsin lights but is unique in being the lone Apostle lighthouse built of brownstone. Built on a red, rocky shore, the dwelling has been likened to a gingerbread house. The light tower has two shapes. The lower portion is four-sided while the upper half is eight-sided, with a focal plane sixty feet above Lake Superior. Light was provided by a fourth-order Fresnel lens that burned a kerosene lamp, producing its white, fixed character. Other structures that made up the Light station included a boathouse and brick out buildings for oil storage and toilet facilities.

The light was lit for the first time on September 25, 1881. Only two light keepers were stationed here for the duration of its manned years. Charles Lederle served for a decade beginning in 1881. He rescued the crew of the *Prussia*, a wooden steamboat that caught fire near the light in the autumn of 1885. Emmanuel Luick served a much longer tenure, from 1892 until 1921, when the lighthouse became the first automated station in the Apostles. A clockwork acetylene-powered light later replaced the human keepers. The light's maintenance became the responsibility of the keeper at nearby Raspberry Island, seven miles to the east.

The keepers and their families on Sand Island were not as cut off from society as some other Apostles keepers. Early in the 1900s the island was populated year-round by commercial fishermen and farmers. There were community events to attend with the other hundred or so island inhabitants who lived in East Bay, two miles from the lighthouse. But economic changes saw a decline in Sand Island's population and by the middle 1940s only a handful of residents remained.

Lightkeepers were required to keep a written logbook of their daily activities associated with the light. Fortunately the Sand Island logs survived and are a valuable historic reference for lighthouse life. Much can be learned about the everyday life of lightkeepers and their families from the Sand Island keeper's log as well as others of nearly a century ago. In addition to their lighthouse duties, Emmanuel and his wife Ella Luick were occupied with various other chores. A garden included potatoes, corn, lettuce, and peas. Berry picking was a favorite activity with currants, raspberries, strawberries, blueberries, blackberries, and cherries available. They raised chickens in a coop and netted fish (trout, herring, burbot, and suckers) to supplement their income. Mr. Luick also hunted wild game and shot at owls and hawks he believed were troublemakers. Wood cutting and chopping seemed to be nearly a daily activity. Reading mail and newspapers was an important pastime that kept them connected to the outside world. Bad weather was more common here than one might think, including many days of fog and rain, snow in the fall, ice and snow into early June, and golf-ball-size hail all during the shipping season, which ran from May into late November or early December.

Ella Luick was only sixteen when she married Emmanuel. Much is known about her and the contribution she made to the running the Sand Island Light. She was a talented young woman who knew how to use a sewing machine and was schooled in music. Her descriptive log book entries indicate that she was a better writer than her husband. Ella Luick at times found life at Sand Island quite lonely. The loneliness that could be an integral part of a lightkeeper's life was put into written words quite nicely by Mrs. Luick. Late in the season in November of 1898, for example, Ella Luick wrote of her boredom: "Mr. Luick hasn't anything to do so he can help me do nothing."

Ella Luick served as assistant keeper at Sand Island Light from the late 1890s into the next century. Many times a trip to the mainland by her keeper husband could last for several days. It then became her responsibility to run the lighthouse. The United States Lighthouse Service officially recognized her as an assistant keeper at Sand Island.

By the time she was 26, in May 1905, Ella Luick left the island and her husband, never to return. They divorced in 1906. Mr. Luick married a second time, to Hattie Oramill Buck (she went by the name of Oramill) and they spent another decade keeping the light. Oramill and Emmanuel had four children, but only two survived childhood.

Sand Island Light was witness to the sinking of the three-thousand-ton iron ore carrier *Sevona* on September 2, 1905. The *Sevona*, a bulk freighter, more than a hundred yards in length, was one of the larger vessels of its day. During a blinding severe storm, the steel steamer collided with Sand Island Shoal, one and a half miles northeast of the lighthouse,

Sand Island Lighthouse

and broke apart. Keeper Luick's log-book contained his eyewitness account of the disaster. The ship carried twenty-four people including four women. The captain and six other sailors perished, despite desperate pleas for help, while attempting to reach Sand Island on a makeshift raft. The Sand Island lightkeeper was involved in recovering many bodies of the unlucky crew, some washing ashore on the island.

After Sand Island's light was automated in 1921 it became a summertime retreat for private individuals who leased the lighthouse. This was a common practice for the government, which was then gradually removing itself from the manned lighthouse business. Fortunately, these summer visitors maintained the station with their own funds, preventing it from falling into disrepair.

In the early 1930s a forty-foot-tall steel tower was built to house a modern beacon which also sported a day marker. Located in front of the lighthouse, it remained active until July of 1985 when the Coast Guard removed it by helicopter. The upper portion of the tower today adorns a Bayfield County bar and restaurant.

Current status: Active aid to navigation. The current beacon is an automated solar- powered light located in the original lantern room. The white light flashes every six seconds, has a 60-foot focal plane, and is visible for seven miles. No fog signal. Volunteer lightkeepers, when available, provide guided tours and visitors can climb the 44 steps to the top of the tower.

How to get there: Sand Island Light is accessible from a boat dock on the eastern side of the island. From the East Bay Campground and Ranger Station, the lighthouse is a two-mile hike. If the lake level is not too low and wave conditions are calm, it is possible to tie a boat up to the metal cleats that are imbedded in the rocks surrounding the shoreline immediately adjacent to the lighthouse on the island's north end. Contact the Apostle Islands Cruise Service.

Raspberry Island Lighthouse

*"When a woman marries a lighthouse keeper,
she gives up everything else in the world."*

—Cecelia McLean, wife of Raspberry Island keeper Alexander
McLean. She should have suspected the worst when they spent
their honeymoon on Devils Island!

      The Native American name for this island translates to
"Island of Raspberries." Across the water on the mainland lies
Raspberry Point and Raspberry Bay, where the Raspberry River
enters Lake Superior. Not surprising, many raspberries grow along
the river. The light station was built on the southwest side of the
island in 1863 to signalize the west channel via the Apostles to ports
east and south (Superior-Duluth, Bayfield, and Ashland). Growth in
Lake Superior trade and the development of the cities of Superior
and Duluth made this light a necessity. The light, equipped with oil
lamps, first saw activity in 1864. The two-story white clapboard
dwelling and square wooden tower stand forty-five feet tall. A fifth-
order Fresnel lens with flash panels on a revolving turntable produced Raspberry Island Light's characteristic white flash. Its focal
plane was approximately eighty feet above the lake level. A red brick
fog signal building, originally equipped with a steam whistle, was
added in 1902, as well as a tramway for raising supplies to the top of

*Many of the duties at Light sta-
tions were quite mundane. The
1928 keeper's log from
Raspberry Island illustrates the varied,
routine, and oftentimes monotonous
workload of a lightkeeper.*
    *June 4 Painted dome and deck of
tower lantern.*
    June 8 Painted fog signal building.
    *June 16 Painted the back portion
of woodshed and outhouse and
closeline posts.*
    *July 12 Taking apart the old stair-
way, which was blown down the
bank by heavy squall.*
    July 16 Repaired roof of dwelling.
    *July 24 Worked on cement walks,
leveling up.*

the steep bank. Extra personnel were added at this station in 1906 and the keeper's quarters were then remodeled into a complex to make room for two assistants.

From 1885 until 1892 Francis Jacker was keeper here. He had requested an assistant on several occasions. He chose to have his family live on the mainland, so the responsibility for maintaining the light was solely his. His being alone, however, caused a near catastrophe. During a windstorm in the autumn of 1887, Jacker went to the boat dock to move the light station's sailboat to a more sheltered place. Because it was dark he was unable to locate the landing place and drifted to Oak Island, two and a half miles to the southeast. Stranded for three days without food, warm clothing, and fire-building tools, he was finally rescued by a Native American. The economic decision not to have an assistant at Raspberry Island could have cost Francis Jacker his life. By the end of 1887 Jacker's brother, Edward, was named as assistant keeper of Raspberry Island. Later, in 1915, the keeper of this light was once again without an assistant, even though lighthouse duties could take more than a hundred hours of work a week.

Automation came to the Raspberry Island Light Station in 1947. Five years later a light was placed atop a short pole on the bank in front of the light station. Today, the Raspberry Island Lighthouse Museum receives more visitors than those of any other Apostle Island lights. The smallest Apostles isle with a lighthouse, the Raspberry Island Lighthouse and grounds are as well kept as any light in Wisconsin. The keeper's quarters and the white board and red brick outbuildings are historically accurate, as are the grounds, including a vegetable garden and flower beds that once graced the station. The flower beds were considered some of the loveliest on any lighthouse grounds. The station, restored to the era of the 1920s and 1930s, allows visitors to enjoy a snapshot of a lighthouse of seventy years ago. The original fifth-order Fresnel lens, complete with flash panels, is now part of an exhibit at the Madeline Island Historical Museum.

A red clay cliff approximately thirty feet tall surrounds the light and had been steadily eroding away. Congress appropriated nearly four million dollars for bluff stabilization and other improvements here and at Outer Island in 1998. The stabilization efforts were undertaken recently and the National Park Service will continue to monitor the situation. Without this care it is feared that the lighthouse will be in jeopardy in a decade or two.

11

Current status: Original tower is inactive. Currently a modern solar-powered beacon atop a steel pole stands in front of the brick fog signal building. It displays a flashing white light every 2.5 seconds with a 58-foot focal plane, visible for seven miles. No fog signal. Special lighthouse cruises are offered during the summer months. Guided tours of the station are available.

How to get there: Accessible by boat. The station has a wooden dock on the southwest side of the island with 74 steps to the top of an old tramway. Contact the Apostle Islands Cruise Service.

Devils Island Lighthouse

Devils Island is the northernmost point in Wisconsin. The island was named by Native Americans who thought this place was evil, their name for it translating to "Evil Spirit Island." Ghostly sounds are created when the combined wind and water of Lake Superior slam into the sandstone sea caves, carved by nature over the centuries. The accompanying cliffs tower several stories high. Kayakers particularly enjoy this area. A shallow bar, Devils Island Shoal rests approximately one and a half miles east of the island.

This was the last "precious stone" added to the necklace of lights on the various isles of the Apostles. In 1891 a temporary wood light tower, sixty-seven feet tall, was constructed on the northern end of the island. A fourth-order Fresnel lens that was fueled by a lard oil lamp was first lit in the autumn of 1891. Producing an alternating white and red color, the light could be seen for approximately nineteen miles in clear weather. At that time a two-story brick Queen Anne-style keeper's quarters and fog signal building were also completed. Devils Island Light was a strategic beacon, located at the most critical turning point in the busy shipping lanes heading upbound and downbound from the Superior area. Captains made final course alterations in the vicinity of this light. Ships swarmed in the area of the Apostles in the early 1900s. In 1903 a count of ships in view of the Devils Island Light totaled 120 in a single day!

In 1897 the light was rebuilt as a white skeletal iron tower. It was not lit until 1901, however, because there was a delay in obtaining the more powerful third-order Fresnel lens from France to place atop the eighty-two-foot steel tower. The taller tower and stronger lens increased the light's visibility to twenty-two miles. A two-story dwelling for the assistant keeper was also added. In the summer, the lantern was covered with red panels to differentiate it from others in the area. The distinctive flashing red beacon was a significant marker in the Apostle-Superior shipping lanes. In the winter the red panes of Plexiglas were removed and the light became a flashing white beacon. The glass panels in the lens room have a diamond shaped pattern. Explanations for this distinct design include possible extra support for the lantern room glass or to minimize light interference compared to horizontal or vertical bars.

Several notable events took place at Devils Island Light. The station was the first in the Apostles to be equipped with radio communication. In 1978 it became the last of the Apostle lights to be automated. In 1989, after nearly nine decades of faithful service, the U.S. Coast Guard removed the Fresnel lens, which was then in need of repair. The old French lens was restored by the National Park Service and placed back in the tower in the summer of 1992. The event was treated as a homecoming of sorts; the Fresnel lens was back atop Devils Island Light Station where it belonged. Sadly the restored Fresnel is there for historic purposes only. Its replacement is a modern solar powered light mounted outside the lantern room on the exterior gallery. The Coast Guard deemed the modern lens to be more efficient and economical. This is the only light remaining in the Apostles with a Fresnel lens.

All Apostle Island light stations closed each December, at the end of the Lake Superior shipping season, opening again the following spring. Sometimes the light stations maintained "winter lights," battery-powered beacons attached to the outside of the regular lantern room.

> **M**ost keepers stationed on remote islands waited for a lighthouse tender ship to take them back to the mainland at the end of the shipping season. One year the keeper at Devils Island walked across frozen Lake Superior—more than nine miles, if he walked a straight line!
>
>

Current status: Active aid to navigation. Red light flashes every ten seconds. Focal plane of 100 feet, visible for 15 miles. No fog signal. Devils Island Light continues to be the only one in the Apostles that flashes a red beacon. National Park Service volunteer lightkeepers provide guided tours from mid-June through Labor Day.

How to get there: Accessible by boat. Dock at Devils Island's south end and trek approximately one mile to the lighthouse complex. There is also a rock landing near the lighthouse on the islands' north end, which is accessible when the weather is calm. Contact the Apostle Islands Cruise Service.

13

Devils Island Lighthouse

Outer Island Lighthouse

"Tower is shaking very bad."

—Log entry of keeper Klaas Hamringa, May 10, 1916, during a particularly fierce Lake Superior storm.

High atop the northern cliff of Outer Island stands its namesake lighthouse. Signalizing the most northeastern limit of the Apostle Islands, Outer Island was named because of its remote location as the most distant island from the mainland of all the Apostles. The Native American name *Gachiishquaguindag Miniss* means "the furthermost island." It is also the largest Apostles isle with a lighthouse, and the second tallest beacon in the islands. Built in 1874 on a forty-foot red clay bluff high above Lake Superior, Outer Island Light guided ships heading into Superior and Duluth when shipments of grain and lumber were increasing. The light also warns of Outer Island Shoal, which lies directly north of the island.

A smooth, white brick, conical tower stands 90 feet tall, 130 feet above the level of Lake Superior. The panorama from the lantern room is breathtaking. Originally a third-order Fresnel lens graced this robust light, producing a powerful white flashing beam that could be seen by sailors twenty-one miles away in good weather. The upper portion near the top of the tower is very ornate, technically called bracketed Italianate style, which was quite popular during this time period. Outer Island possessed two fog signals. The keeper's home, a three-story red brick structure, is attached to the towering light. At one time the light station also consisted of a boathouse with a pier and a motorized tramway to haul supplies up the steep cliffs.

This remote island is unprotected by other landmasses and bears the full brunt of Lake Superior's ferocious gale winds and nor'easters. Strong storms have actually caused the tower to sway and have, over time, heavily eroded the banks immediately north of the light. Rough weather forced the relocation over the years of the fog signal building as well as replacement of the motorized tramway. The elements also took their toll on boathouses, several of them being removed by Mother Nature over the years.

The storm of September 2, 1905, which had claimed the steamer *Sevona* off Sand Island earlier in the day, also sunk the schooner-barge *Pretoria* off Outer Island. Loaded with tons of iron ore, the wooden ship foundered slightly more than a mile northeast of the island in one of the worst Lake Superior storms (a nor'easter) in many a year. The ill-fated ship was only five years old and was a tremendously large vessel for its time, over three hundred feet in length. As the lake slowly chewed the vessel apart, the crew took to a lifeboat and abandoned ship. The lighthouse keeper at the time, sixty-year-old John Irvine, was able to assist five of the crew to safety. An equal number of the crew was not as lucky and perished, including an African-American cook.

Outer Island was one of the more desolate light stations in the Apostles. Isolation and no frills marked the character of its earliest days. In today's terms it was primitive living, lacking electricity, telephone, radio, and refrigeration. The daughter of Otto Olson, keeper for nine years, recalled that her father went to Bayfield once a month for supplies. At most other times the family was detached from much of the world. The remoteness of Outer Island Light can be illustrated by the following quote from *The Northern Lights*, by noted lighthouse historian Charles K. Hyde: "Late one shipping season, the keeper died, and it was two weeks before his body could be removed!"

Electricity eventually came to Outer Island in the 1930s. In 1961, the station became fully automated. The Fresnel lens no longer sits atop the lantern room, having been replaced by a modern beacon.

Leaving an Apostle Island Light station at the end of the shipping season was often hazardous due to the unpredictability of Lake Superior weather conditions. In December of 1919 the lighthouse tender ship Marigold plucked keepers from Raspberry, Sand, and Outer Islands just as supplies were running out. When the Marigold reached her home port of Duluth her supply of coal was nearly depleted and ice reached two miles from shore. The captain and his men forged their way through the ice to safe harbor.

15

Outer Island Lighthouse

Current status: Active aid to navigation. Today the light is a modern plastic lens powered by solar panels. White light flashes every ten seconds. 130-foot focal plane, visible for 15 miles. No fog signal.

Congress appropriated nearly four million dollars for bluff stabilization and other improvements here and at Raspberry Island in 1998. Badly needed stabilization efforts were recently undertaken and the National Park Service will continue to monitor the banks. Without intervention it is likely that the lighthouse complex will succumb to erosion.

Special cruises offer views of the station seasonally. Volunteer lightkeepers provide guided tours mid-June through Labor Day.

How to get there: One of the least visited lighthouses in the Apostles because of its remoteness, the island has a cement dock on its north side and is accessible only by boat. Climb the 98 steps to the top of the cliff. Contact the Apostle Islands Cruise Service.

Michigan Island Old Lighthouse

*"Mother always gave the U.S. Lighthouse Service Inspectors a bouquet, or if we had fresh berries,
she'd give them a gift of that to take back. But they always admired her flowers."*

—Keeper Ed Lane's daughter, Edna Lane Sauer, recalling her childhood days on Michigan Island.

The original Michigan Island Lighthouse was a colossal construction mistake. The oldest light in the Apostle Islands, Michigan Island marks the eastern boundary and northern course to the early ports of Bayfield, Washburn, and La Pointe on Madeline Island. Later it would serve to guide vessels to the bustling port of Ashland. The lighthouse was to have been constructed on Long Island to the south to guide mariners through the southern channel, the eastern approach to the Apostle Islands. A construction crew from Milwaukee, apparently due to a misinterpretation, built the lighthouse here in 1857 on the southern side of Michigan Island in error!

Composed of coarse stone, the story-and-a-half dwelling and attached tower are stucco, painted white. This light is of a plain style, reminding one of lighthouses found on the Atlantic Coast. First lit in the spring of 1857, the black lantern stands just sixty-four feet above the ground but double that height above Lake Superior. Later it would be determined that this light was too short. When officials realized the error of the location of this inaugural Apostles light, the Old Michigan Lighthouse was closed in 1858 after only one year of operation. The lantern was removed and used at Windmill Point on Lake St. Clair between lakes Huron and Erie. The La Pointe Light, the original location on Long Island to the south where the first Apostle Island light was supposed to be built, was then constructed.

In 1869 the government appropriated several thousand dollars to restore the Old Michigan Island Light and repair the building when it was determined that a light here would still be helpful to sailors piloting on the eastern shore of the Apostles to such ports as Bayfield and La Pointe. Because the structure had been plundered for bricks, windows, and other materials during the eleven years it was unused, a massive renovation was necessary before the light could be operated again. The light boasted a three-and-a-half order Fresnel lens and was powered by an incandescent oil vapor lamp. An additional Michigan Island tower was erected in 1929 and the original Old Michigan Fresnel lens was placed in the new tower. The old lighthouse was darkened for a second and perhaps final time.

Several notable keepers called the Old Michigan Island Light home. Ed Lane and his family first lived in the "Old Lighthouse" for twenty-seven years before the new, taller tower and lovely brick home were built. He held the position of keeper on Michigan Island for the longest tenure of anyone stationed at one Apostles lighthouse—thirty-seven years. Mr. Lane retired at the age of sixty-nine.

The Old Michigan Lighthouse tower closed annually with the end of the shipping season, usually in December. Winter could be brutal in the Apostles. Occasionally, however, keepers and their families in the late 1800s would overwinter at the lighthouse, even though the waters surrounding the Apostle Isles were frozen. Life centered primarily around maintenance and housekeeping chores. The family would sometimes ice fish to supplement their food supply.

Current status: Inactive; presently no lens adorns the tower. This station also can be toured seasonally with a volunteer keeper. The building and tower are in the process of being restored. Renovation work on the brickwork of the building and surface work on the tower has taken place over the last few summers. Much additional work needs to be done as funding permits.

How to get there: Accessible by boat. A dock can be found on the southern shore of the island. Contact the Apostle Islands Cruise Service.

Michigan Island Light Tower

The tallest lighthouse in Wisconsin, the second tower on Michigan Island was erected in 1929 after lying idle on the island for a decade. This skeletal and cylindrical tower, built in 1869, had served as a beacon at Schooner Ledge on the Delaware River in Pennsylvania where it was declared unnecessary. It was dismantled and transported in sections to Michigan Island in 1919. Like its predecessor, this newer model guided ships along the North and South Channels around Madeline Island to the ports of Ashland, Bayfield, and La Pointe. First lit on October 29, 1929, this 112-foot iron skeleton is the loftiest and most recent of the Apostle lights. Michigan Island holds the distinction of having both the oldest and newest of the Apostles Islands lighthouses. Nearly double the height of the Old Michigan Lighthouse, the Fresnel lens was boosted another fifty feet higher above Lake Superior.

A new, red brick, three-bedroom, two-story bungalow for the keeper was added to the Michigan Island complex at this time. In addition, a building for an electric generator to power the light (as well as other power needs), a fog signal, a privy, a radio beacon, and a lift motor for a tramway to transport rations up the sheer rock were built. Today, 123 steps will take you up from the boat dock, and an additional 138 stairs will take you to the lantern room. The outstanding view from the deck outside the lantern room is well worth the trek and the aching in your leg muscles!

The Lane family, keeper Ed, his wife Elizabeth, and their children, called Michigan Island home for much of their lives. The compound featured cherry, crabapple, and pear trees, a vegetable garden, and flower plantings. A mammoth evergreen tree that harbored nesting bald eagles, bordered the lighthouse property. Clearly a man ahead of the times, Keeper Lane used to share a portion of his catch of fish with the eagles.

The Michigan Tower was automated in 1941. The original three-and-a-half-order Fresnel lens was removed in 1972 and can be viewed at the Apostle Islands Visitors Center in Bayfield.

> *From keeper Ed Lane's logbook entry of October 29, 1929: "Put window shades and worked in old tower. Started up new tower at sunset. Everything in good shape, but station looked odd, the old tower being dark for the first time in navigation in 60 years."*
>
> ⚓

19

Current status: Active aid to navigation. White light flashes every six seconds. 170-foot focal plane, visible for 11 miles. No fog signal. When volunteer keepers are in residence both of the towers are open for inspection. Special cruises offer views of the station in season.

How to get there: Accessible by boat. A dock can be found on the southern shore of the island. Contact the Apostle Islands Cruise Service.

20

Michigan Island Light Tower

La Pointe Lighthouse on Long Island

The La Pointe Lighthouse holds the distinction of being the longest continuously operating light in the Apostles group at 141 years; it just keeps going and going and going. Long Island comprises the last two miles of a nearly seven-mile intermittent stretch of land originally known as Chequamegon Point. At one time Long Island was connected to the main thread of land that comprises Chequamegon Point. It became separated from the main landmass in the early 1820s. In the mid- to late 1890s, Chequamegon Bay was the second busiest port on the Great Lakes. The city of La Pointe on Madeline Island was a central port for many industries and principal cargoes included furs, iron ore, lumber, sandstone, grain and fish. Long Island was the final island added to the Apostle Islands National Lakeshore.

Some discrepancies exist as to the proposed location of the first lighthouse in the Apostles. Congress actually authorized a lighthouse at La Pointe on Madeline Island in 1852. However the majority of ships traveling to this port entered from the east. It was determined that Long Island to the south was a better choice for the Apostle Island's inaugural light. Ships using the ports of Bayfield and La Pointe navigated a shipping lane known as the South Channel, which bisected Madeline Island on the north and Long Island on the south. The light's location was essential, marking the entrance to the La Pointe harbor on Madeline Island, hence the light's name.

La Pointe became the second lighthouse put into service in the Apostle Islands, although it should have been the first. It was discovered that the light intended for Long Island was built on Michigan Island in 1857 in error. It is likely that this mistake cost the builders dearly, probably forcing them to construct the La Pointe Light at no additional cost to the government. This light station, located on the northern side Long Island, played a significant part in the improvement of shipping in this small section of Lake Superior. The original thirty-five-foot tall wooden tower and clapboard keepers quarters were built in 1858 on the island's north side, approximately 1,500 feet east of Long Island's western boundary. The original light was a fixed white beacon.

The initial La Pointe Light proved to be ill-constructed, and an unstable foundation doomed it to a relatively short life. In 1895 a sixty-seven-foot skeletal steel white tower with a central column later supported by braces was built several

Keeper Joseph Sexton served the longest of any of the keepers on Long Island—thirty-two years. Joe grew up with lighthouses; his family farmed on Michigan Island in the 1870s and 1880s. He became acquainted with the keepers there and the thought of working for the U.S. Lighthouse Service appealed to young Joe. He was given the post of second assistant keeper at Outer Island Light Station in 1886 and was promoted to first assistant within a year. In 1889 he rose to the rank of keeper and was dispatched to Long Island where he would remain until 1921. Keeper Joe was the father of eleven children. One can certainly feel for Mrs. Sexton!

21

thousand feet east of the inaugural light and keepers quarters. The fourth-order Fresnel lens from the first lighthouse was placed in the new tower. A white light shown from this beacon. One of the oldest skeletal lighthouses on the Great Lakes, a fog signal building was also part of the La Pointe complex. Near the turn of the twentieth century the keeper of this light also was obligated to tend the Chequamegon Light slightly west of here on the same island. In the early 1920s a radio signal beacon was instituted at La Point Light. The light became automated in 1964.

Like many of the Apostles Isles, Long Island was the scene of another noteworthy shipwreck. A 195-foot-long, three-masted schooner, the *Lucerne*, making her final run of the season, sank off the island on November 17 or 18, 1886, east of La Pointe Light. Piloting one of the sturdiest vessels on the lake, the captain may have been seeking the La Pointe Light and the shelter of Chequamegon Bay when a nor'easter storm claimed the cargo of iron ore and several crewmen. The lightkeeper at La Pointe Light found the ship partially submerged on November 19, 1886, approximately two and a half miles from the lighthouse. He found three corpses on board the wrecked vessel covered with ice. One of the deceased was dressed for bitter weather, wearing heavy underwear and five layers of coats. Another, it was learned, had been taking his first voyage on the *Lucerne*. An additional body soon washed ashore on Long Island. A total of nine sailors perished.

La Pointe Light

Current status: Active aid to navigation. A modern green iso light flashes every six seconds. 70 foot focal plane, visible for eight miles. No fog signal.

How to get there: Accessible only by boat. Long Island currently has no usable docks (the pier on the north end of the island is in need of major repair). The National Park Service, as of the time of this writing, is in the process of rehabilitating the Long Island dock. Once this work is complete, Long Island will once again be accessible. Contact the Apostle Islands Cruise Service.

Chequamegon Point Light

The name Chequamegon (pronounced she-wam'-e-gun by the locals) is related to the structure of the island. Originating from the Native American Ojibwa word *Shagewomekong*, it is believed to mean "long point or strip of land" or "soft beaver dam." Chequamegon Point was home to a commercial fishing operation dating to the late 1800s.

Located on the westernmost tip of Long Island and the Chequamegon isthmus in Chequamegon Bay, the light was built in 1895, and was first lit two years later. This light has a spider-like appearance, and has been likened to a lunar lander. Standing only forty-two feet tall with a thirty-five-foot focal plane, this is the shortest light in the collection of Apostle lighthouses. The white, square, skeletal, four-legged, iron tower originally housed a fourth-order Fresnel lens. The spindly legs were anchored by cement posts reinforced by supporting diagonal struts. The main upper body of the station has a window that affords a splendid view of Chequamegon Bay. The octagonal lantern room was first fired by an oil lamp and sported a fixed white light. A ladder allowed the keeper access to the lamp. The red roof and ventilator ball top off the tower. The light station also exhibited a striking bell fog signal and a boathouse.

The Chequamegon Point Light and La Pointe Light, as well as their fog signals, were tended by the same keeper. A cement walkway, slightly more than a quarter-mile long, linked the two Long Island towers. The Chequamegon and La Pointe Light stations were both automated in 1964. The original Chequamegon Light became deactivated in 1986 and was moved approximately 150 feet further inland by a U.S. Coast Guard helicopter a year later to resist damage from erosion along the shoreline. Ironically, the structure was badly damaged during the move that was supposed to insure its survival. An automated light atop a tubular structure was put into place in 1986. The original lighthouse is on the National Register of Historic Places.

Current status: The old skeletal tower stands idle and had been replaced by a modern tube beacon with a green light that flashes every four seconds, thirty-three-foot focal plane, visible for seven miles. No fog signal. The lights on Long Island are not currently staffed, but the buildings may be viewed from the water.

How to get there: Accessible only by boat. Currently Long Island has no usable docks. (The pier on the north end of the island is in need of major repair). The National Park Service is in the process of rehabilitating the Long Island dock. Once that work is complete, Long Island will once again be accessible. Contact the Apostle Islands Cruise Service.

23

Ashland

Founded in 1854, Ashland was a thriving center for both rail and water transportation of iron ore and lumber shipping in the late nineteenth century and into the twentieth. Situated on the southern shore of Lake Superior on the Chequamegon Bay, the port's ore boat capacity peaked in the years of World War II and declined to a fraction of that by the 1950s. In 1965 ore shipments from the Soo Line ore dock ceased, ending ninety-three years of shipments that began 1872. Ashland continued to be a hub for lumbering traffic well into the twentieth century, even as mills in other cities ceased to operate. An old, giant, iron ore dock stands near the harbor, slowly rusting away. Today, Ashland is nicknamed "Lake Superior's hometown."

Ashland Breakwater Light

Early in the twentieth century, a lighthouse was needed to guide vessels in and out of the booming Ashland harbor. Shallow areas near the light also are a potential hazard to navigation and needed to be marked. Located on the west end of the approximately one-and-one-half-mile-long breakwater out in Chequamegon Bay, the beacon was built in 1914 and first lighted the following year. Massive boulders protect the lighthouse and pier from the ravages of Lake Superior. The light, also known as Chequamegon Bay Breakwater Light, was first illuminated with a fourth-order Fresnel lens. Ashland Breakwater Light is the last remaining notable poured, reinforced, concrete lighthouse of its kind in the United States. The square base of the lighthouse rises to form a tower the shape of a pyramid which then transitions into a circular lantern room. The lantern's glass is diamond-shaped. The lighthouse stands nearly sixty feet above Lake Superior and Chequamegon Bay. While the Coast Guard is charged with the upkeep of the light and tower, the U.S. Army Corps of Engineers is responsible for the maintenance of the breakwater on which the lighthouse rests.

The original Fresnel lens was replaced with a modern beacon many years ago. The light was later fully automated and is now solar powered.

Imagine the view that the keepers of Ashland Light enjoyed from the top of the lantern room. Chequamegon Bay teemed with vessels busily going about their business when Ashland was a bustling port. It must have been quite a sight.

24

I n 1918, ore boats carried more tonnage out of the Ashland harbor than passed through the Panama Canal.

Current status: Active aid to navigation. White light flashes every six seconds, visible for nine miles, 60 foot focal plane. No foghorn.

How to get there: When approaching Ashland from the East, travel 1.8 miles from the city limits to Bay View Park. The lighthouse can be viewed from shore or from a short pier. The Ashland Breakwater Light can be found on the non-continuous breakwater. The only way to achieve a close-up view is by boat.

Following page: Ashland Breakwater Light

Lake Winnebago.

This eastern Wisconsin inland lake borders Appleton and Neenah-Menasha on the north, Oshkosh midway on its western side, and Fond du Lac at its southern tip. Lake Winnebago is part of the Wolf and Fox River systems. The Upper Fox enters Winnebago through Lake Butte des Mortes near Oshkosh and exits at Neenah-Menasha where the Lower Fox continues northward on its way to the southern end of Green Bay.

The name Winnebago is derived from the Native American tribe who settled this area. It is the largest interior lake in Wisconsin, covering 215 square miles. The length of Winnebago is roughly thirty miles, its width varies from five to ten miles, and the maximum depth is only twenty-one feet. Despite this shallowness, Winnebago can still be quite dangerous in bad weather.

Lake Winnebago and her connecting rivers have been a valuable resource to this part of Wisconsin for hundreds of years. Joliet and Marquette traveled these water "highways" in the seventeenth century. They were part of the commercial route between French Canada and the Gulf of Mexico. Grinding mills utilized the waters of the "Big Lake." Later, lumbering became a principal activity, lasting through the 1800s. Winnebago ice was also an important winter commodity. Additionally, recreational boating has been a mainstay for tourists and locals for decades. The lake continues to be popular today for its sport fishing and other water recreation activities.

Parts of the Fox system are a workhorse river with many industries and commercial docks along its route. The navigation season on Lake Winnebago runs from approximately the beginning of May through October. The four lighthouses here are some of the newest in the state.

27

Seagull at sunrise

Neenah

In the mid 1850s a massive lighthouse was located at the head of the Menasha channel on the very northern limits of Lake Winnebago. It had a short life, however, and was reduced to ruins by 1880. An envisioned waterway linking the Fox and Wisconsin Rivers never materialized at that time, so the light was not considered to be cost-effective. The abandoned light would become a gathering place for skating parties and as a shelter for fishermen before a fire gutted it in 1879. Nautical charts of today still feature Lighthouse Reef on the very northernmost end of Lake Winnebago. Water depths of only two to three feet are common a half-mile off the Neenah-Menasha shoreline.

Neenah Lighthouse

A quiet, beautiful scenic 3.25-acre waterfront park, Kimberly Point Park in Neenah, on Lake Winnebago's northwestern edge, is home to one of four present-day Lake Winnebago lighthouses. Approximately 150 feet west of the Point was an aged tree known as the "Old Council Tree." It is here that Native Americans and European settlers would rendezvous and "hold council." The tree was cut down in 1885 in order to make improvements in the Fox River.

The Neenah Lighthouse may never have been built in Kimberly Point Park if not for the forward thinking of Helen Kimberly Stuart. Mrs. Stuart originally donated this site to Neenah's park system in 1929 as her gift to the community. Clearly a trailblazer, she was involved heavily in community issues in the 1930s and 1940s and her accomplishments were many. She was the first woman elected to the Neenah Board of Education, and the first woman to serve on Neenah's City Council, Plans Commission, and Library Board. She became the first woman to run for Mayor of Neenah. She founded the Neenah League of Women Voters, was President of the State League of Women Voters, and

Neenah Lighthouse

was appointed to the Board of Regents of the University of Wisconsin. Mrs. Stuart successfully battled the Kimberly-Clark Company, the largest paper company in town. Its president, F. J. Sensenbrenner, had planned to buy all the land forming the Point and build a million-dollar estate on land that was known at that time as Park Point and thought to be forever public. No one worked with as much energy as Mrs. Stuart to preserve Point Park and the road allowing access to it, Lake Shore Drive. Mr. Sensenbrenner did eventually built his home, but on the opposite side of Lake Winnebago. Helen Kimberly Stuart had triumphed. The land remained public, and in addition Mrs. Stuart donated four additional parcels to expand the size of the park. She also funded its maintenance for many years to come, and financed the planting of elm and flowering crabapple trees, some of which survive to this day. The park is named for Mrs. Stuart's father, John A. Kimberly.

Discussions about erecting a lighthouse at the confluence of the Fox River and Lake Winnebago first began in 1939. The Flour Brothers Construction Company of Oshkosh completed construction in 1945. The lighthouse is named for James C. Kimberly who donated the funds for the project in 1944. It was also proposed that a comfort station (restroom) be built in the form of a lighthouse on the northwestern side of the lake.

The tower is constructed of brick and block. The upper tower section has several windows along with a framed steel and glass top portion that houses the beacon. Total height of the structure is thirty-nine and a half feet. There are twin porches on each side of the base, forming a patio.

Neenah Lighthouse is a distinguishing landmark and functions as a beacon welcoming boaters going to and from Lake Winnebago from the Fox River. The light is controlled automatically by a timer and is operational during the navigational season, which runs from early May through October. It is considered an official navigational aid. The upper portion housing the light is not open to the public and no tours are given. Handicapped accessible restrooms are available and a handicapped accessible fishing deck, added in 1991, increases the usefulness of the light and park for everyone. Playground equipment and picnic facilities may also be found here.

Current status: Active aid to navigation.

How to get there: Located on Lakeshore Ave. at the end of Wisconsin Ave. in Kimberly Point Park. From the north, on U.S. 41, exit at highway 114 (Winneconne Ave.). Stay on Hwy. 114 for 1.2 miles until you reach Commercial St. Turn left onto Commercial St. and proceed 0.3 of a mile until you reach Wisconsin Ave. Turn right onto Wisconsin and go 0.9 of a mile, until you come to Lakeshore Ave.; turn left at Lakeshore. Go another 0.5 of a mile and you will see the sign for Kimberly Point Park. For further information contact the Neenah Park and Recreation Department, P.O. Box 426, Neenah, WI 54957-0426.

Asylum Bay Lighthouse

The old Asylum Bay Lighthouse stands idle, a lonely sentinel in a once busy area known as Asylum Point. Located several miles north of Oshkosh on Winnebago's western coast, the Wisconsin Conservation Commission (WCC) and federal Works Projects Administration (WPA) were involved in the development of this area in the 1930s and 1940s. The lighthouse, constructed in 1940, stood guard on an artificial island once known as Lighthouse Island and Picnic Point. Asylum Point separates North and South Asylum Bays. The main column of the lighthouse stands twenty-four feet high and has a circumference of eight feet at the base, which tapers to six feet near the top. Several rectangular windows, now boarded up, adorn the length of the brick tower. A large door sits at the base. The structure is topped with a seven-foot-tall cupola. Years ago a flagpole crowned the lighthouse, raising its total height to forty-two feet.

The original island was primarily marshland which, when filled in, measured two football fields in length and about seventy-five feet wide. The island, with numerous trees, shrubs, and flowers, was a popular spot for picnickers. Several open-air fireplaces also were available. A wooden bridge once connected Lighthouse Island to the mainland.

A fishpond was created from the dredging of a channel, and a rough fish removal program for Lake Winnebago was centered here. Carp and sheepshead were removed and sold to markets in Chicago and New York. The rough fish harvest averaged a million pounds annually. The Asylum Bay Lighthouse marked this fish operations headquarters, guiding fishermen as they returned to shore at night. It also served to mark a refuge for any boats caught on Lake Winnebago in stormy weather. The headquarters was a hub of activity, serving as the site for boat-building, barge traffic, and fish trapping equipment. When this entire area was being developed, a significant Native American burial ground was discovered.

There were problems obtaining a license to operate the light and it was never electrified. The light was lit with a kerosene lantern to guide those who harvested the rough fish. A flashing beacon with a range of a dozen miles in good weather sent its light out over the lake. It is unknown when this light ceased operation.

Current status: No longer operational. Portions of the old footbridge to the island where the light stands have been removed, but good views are possible from the parking lot across the narrow channel.

How to get there: From the north, take U.S. Highway 41 south until you reach Snell Road. Turn left onto Snell Road. Cross County A, then go 0.3 of a mile to Sherman Road. At this point the road goes only to the left or right. You will see a Wisconsin Department of Natural Resources Headquarters sign. Turn right onto Sherman. Follow Sherman approx. 0.8 of a mile past the Asylum Bay Boat Launch. Follow winding road to Asylum Point and a small parking lot.

Asylum Bay Lighthouse

Oshkosh

The city of Oshkosh was named in honor of the Menominee Chief "Oskosh" (note spelling, with first H missing). The city was settled in 1836 at the site of a former French trading post. Located at the mouth of the Fox River, the waterways around Oshkosh played a vital role in its early development and history. Early on, a trading post and sawmill were established here. A major contributing factor in the early economic success of Oshkosh was its local access to the waters of Lake Winnebago and beyond. Today, many recreational opportunities await Oshkosh citizens and tourists.

Rockwell Lighthouse

Rockwell Lighthouse has been an Oshkosh landmark for nearly nine decades, located on Winnebago's western shore where the Fox River empties into Lake Winnebago. Built in 1909, one old account says the light was used to mark nearby reefs. Much of Lake Winnebago in the general vicinity of the lighthouse is shallow. George Andrews Rockwell, a native of Oshkosh and an architect, drew up plans for the light in 1909, shortly before his death at the age of 41. William Bray, a former Wisconsin State Senator and friend of Rockwell, acquired several parcels of land in 1907 and 1908 that included the fairly isolated point. Mr. Bray built the light after the Rockwell's blueprints were discovered following his death. Records show that Mr. Bray tried but failed to convince the government to erect a lighthouse on the point, so he built the light with his own funds and assumed the cost of upkeep and the responsibility of keeping the light lit. The lighthouse was a part of Mr. Bray's private harbor improvements for his own pleasure boats. He transformed the entire point into a showplace where he entertained friends and colleagues. President William Howard Taft once visited here. In the early 1900s this area was quite isolated and it was

32

Rockwell Lighthouse's ornate top

Rockwell Lighthouse

reported that rainstorms made the roads virtually impassable.

The light also served to signalize the area for shipping on the Fox River and Lake Winnebago during the years when commercial navigation was important in this area. The beacon was considered a government-licensed light, however, after 1917, when commercial traffic became substantial. The government then realized the importance of the light and did pay its expenses for a time. It has been reported that early airplanes also used this light as a guiding beacon before pilot guidance systems became more accurate.

In the years that ensued, the lighthouse and the point of land it occupied were associated with the families that lived there. The lighthouse and surrounding property and point have changed owners many times. The lighthouse and point were normally named for the owners of the land, including Bray (1909), Thompson (1918), and Buckstaff (1940s). All owners were responsible for paying taxes on this private property that contains the light.

In 1917, Thompson's Point Lighthouse (nee Rockwell Lighthouse) was the only government-licensed inland light. When the federal government decreed that the light must be kept lit without interruption, Mrs. Thompson was appointed keeper. She held a license for the lighthouse for many years.

Rockwell Lighthouse is one of the most ornate of all Wisconsin lights, with white and cream-colored stucco walls and delicate black ironwork. Numerous windows line the tower and a short staircase leads to a doorway at the light's base. Its total height is approximately forty-two feet. During the late 1950s the light was no longer lit and the tower fell into disrepair for a number of years. In the mid-1980s the street and area immediately surrounding the light were renovated to allow more privacy for the owners of the property and to protect the light from vandals. The light was restored and re-lit in the summer of 1986 by the owners of the property. A park-like setting now gives this historic beacon more security. The light sits on a miniature concrete and grass island. A copper plaque at the base of the light reads: Rockwell Light, George Andrews Rockwell, architect, 1909.

Current status: This privately owned and operated light is in a residential area. The light may easily be viewed from the street. It continues to show the way for recreational users of Lake Winnebago who are guided by its fixed red light. The beacon operates year-round and is controlled by a photo sensor that automatically turns the light on day or night when the sky darkens. The owners are listed with the U.S. Coast Guard as the official lighthouse keepers. For more information contact the Oshkosh Public Library, Historian, 106 Washington Ave., Oshkosh, WI 54901.

How to get there: From the north or south, take Main St. (highway 45), into downtown Oshkosh. Turn right (east) onto Merritt Ave. Drive 0.4 of a mile to Bowen St.; turn right (south) on Bowen. Go 0.6 of a mile to Bay Shore Drive. Turn left (east) onto Bay Shore, proceed 0.5 of a mile until the road makes a sharp left turn just before a home with a large stone wall in front of it. The address is 6 Lake St. The lighthouse will be on your right. This light is on private property. Please respect! We asked permission to step into an adjacent yard to better photograph the light and the neighbors gladly said yes.

Fond du Lac

Fond du Lac translated fittingly means, "end of the lake." In the early 1800s Fond du Lac was the site of a French trading post. Later it nearly was named the capital of the new state of Wisconsin. Fond du Lac County is home to rich farmland and stone quarries.

Fond du Lac Lighthouse

This decorative eight-sided light tower is a picturesque landmark well known to Fond du Lac residents and visitors. Locals know this light as Lakeside Park Lighthouse. Visitors to the scenic park also know it as a friendly welcoming beacon. Situated at the entrance to the Fond du Lac harbor, marina, and Yacht Club, at the southernmost end of Lake Winnebago, buoys also mark the channel. The structure replaced an ordinary red light that previously marked the harbor entrance.

This lighthouse, the brainchild of Fond du Lac lumberman W. J. Nuss, was built entirely with donated building materials and private funds from Nuss and others. The cornerstone was laid on July 10, 1933, with much pomp and circumstance. The white, Cape Cod-style tower stands approximately fifty-six feet tall and measures twelve feet in diameter. The base is composed of stone. Funds to purchase a light to top the tower were raised by the local yacht club, which conducted excursions on Lake Winnebago at the time. A stairway allows the public to climb to the open walkway atop the tower. The observation platform is forty-four feet from the ground. A gorgeous panoramic view of Lake Winnebago and the nearby harbor rewards your climb of seventy-two steps.

In the early 1960s the tower was closed to the public because it was deemed unsafe. During windy conditions the tower could be felt swaying. Later in that decade the local Optimists Club and the city of Fond du Lac appropriated funds to rebrace the interior of the tower and to replace the stairs, floors, and roof. The interior walls, which displayed years of graffiti, were left intact while the outside received a new coat of white paint. A celebration commemorating the newly renovated tower was held on July 3, 1968. Mounted on a boulder on the lighthouse grounds is a plaque that reads, "Saved 1967, Restored 1993. Fond du Lac Evening Optimist Club."

Today, boaters still utilize the red light atop the white tower by lining it up with a light behind the boathouses, similar to a range light system. Many swallows nest under the viewing platform. The grounds surrounding the lighthouse are neatly landscaped, boasting many colorful plantings. Tours are self-guided. The tower is closed in the winter. Lakeside Park encompasses four hundred acres along Lake Winnebago. In addition to boating, there are many opportunities to picnic, relax, watch the kids at the playgrounds, or take a stroll around the scenic grounds.

Fond du Lac Lighthouse

Current status: Active aid to navigation. A red flashing light is operational during the boating season, May through October. The tower is open from 6 a.m. until sunset.

How to get there: Located in the city of Fond du Lac at the north end of Main St. (Hwy. 175). Follow signs to Lakeside Park. Contact the Fond du Lac Convention and Visitors Bureau, 19 W. Scott St., Fond du Lac, WI 54935.

Lake Michigan.

Lake Michigan. Many names designated this expanse of water. One derivation has its roots in an Algonquian phrase meaning "big water." Another Native American tribe's words *Michi Gami* meant "great lake." The French explorer Jean Nicolet was probably the first European to visit the lake in the early part of the seventeenth century. In the mid-1600s the lake was known to the French as *Lac de Puans*.

Lake Michigan is the second largest of the Great Lakes by volume and the only one located entirely within the borders of the United States. The sixth largest lake on earth containing fresh water, it discharges into Lake Huron through the Straits of Mackinac. Lake Michigan is part of a waterway that extends eastward to the Atlantic Ocean and southward via the Mississippi River to the Gulf of Mexico. In excess of 300 miles in length and more than 115 miles wide in places, Lake Michigan's periphery of more than 1,600 miles of shoreline envelops more than 22,000 square miles. It is a vital link that connects the heartland of the Midwest to the Atlantic Ocean and the world.

Agricultural and industrial products have been transported via this waterway for several hundred years. The westward movement of the developing nation slowly opened Lake Michigan. With the opening of the Erie Canal in 1825 linking Albany and Buffalo, the Welland Canal connecting Lakes Ontario and Erie in 1829, and the canal at Sault Ste. Marie in 1855, Great Lakes trade blossomed. Lumber, grain, fuels, and ore moved from the Midwest to the East Coast while

Freighter in Milwaukee Harbor

manufactured goods moved in the opposite direction. Water travel during this time was significantly more economical than use of the relatively primitive road system. Lumber, fish, furs, stone, iron ore, and coal were the most prominent products transported via water in Wisconsin from about the 1850s into the beginning of the next century.

Lake Michigan poses significant dangers to ships. Freshwater waves are less compact than their saltwater counterparts, and therefore have sharper edges than the flow of the ocean. As many as two thousand ships have been lost on Lake Michigan.

Since the middle of the nineteenth century, Lake Michigan has had more lights than any of the other Great Lakes. For some reason, almost all red Great Lakes lighthouses are found on Lake Michigan.

Bay of Green Bay

The bay of Green Bay is an indentation in the western side of Lake Michigan. The name stems from the algae blooms that impart a pea-soup green color to these waters in the summertime. Historically, many Native American tribes occupied this area. Jean Nicolet is believed to be the first European to explore Wisconsin, in 1634. A major settlement flourished here, a fur-trading post was its commercial center. A mission for the French explorers Louis Joliet and Jacques Marquette was founded here in the mid-1600s as they made their way westward to discover the mighty Mississippi River. The first permanent European settlement in Wisconsin, Green Bay would later be proclaimed the "Gateway to the Great Waterway." The British controlled the community from the mid-1700s until after the War of 1812. In what would later become Brown County, the State of Wisconsin had its birth. Originally a vast wilderness, the Green Bay area was very early in its history a premier fishing area and a center for lumbering. Cleared lands fostered agriculture. Eventually commercial

Fishing boat on Green Bay

products of all kinds flowed in and out of the bustling harbor. Later, papermaking fueled the regional economy.

During the 1800s the Port of Green Bay was one of the busiest on the Great Lakes. Upwards of seven thousand vessels, including sailing ships and steamboats, passed to and from the bay during this time. Like other areas of Wisconsin undergoing expansion and growth, lighthouses here were a natural response to the need for safer water travel. Multiple lighthouses were eventually needed because the original maritime channel was exceedingly crooked, and difficult to navigate even in daylight.

Presently, lower (southern) Green Bay is littered with several dozen light beacons and buoys not qualifying as lighthouses. They do, however, serve to guide the mariner safely in and out of the harbor. Green Bay normally freezes over by late December or early January.

Southern Green Bay is at the mouth of the Fox River. This dominant waterway is named for the Fox Indians, one of several groups of Native Americans who settled this region. The Fox River system was the door to the interior of Wisconsin, connecting to the Wisconsin River and eventually the Mississippi River. Its importance cannot be overestimated. The Fox River helped form a link to the Mississippi and the Gulf of Mexico.

Menominee North Pier Light

Actually a State of Michigan beacon, the Menominee North Pier Light serves in a dual capacity to guard the combined harbor of Menominee, Michigan, and Marinette, Wisconsin. This light stands at the confluence of the Menominee River and Green Bay. The river connection was a vital one, carrying Native Americans, fur traders, explorers, and missionaries. Lumbering was the chief business in the 1800s in Marinette and Menominee, with white pine felled and taken to the numerous sawmills in the area. Extensive iron ore deposits were also mined. The city of Marinette is reportedly named after a Native American of the same name who was the wife of one of the early fur traders in the area.

A light at this location dates to 1877. The original structure was a light-colored, conical tower several stories tall, topped by a dark lantern room. A large building, housing a fog signal, was situated immediately behind the lighthouse on a wooden dock. The current structure was built in 1927. An extensive raised, metal catwalk, once present, no longer exists. A doorway on the back of the light, where the catwalk connected, remains. Today the red signature, eight-sided metal tower sits atop a large, square, concrete base on the end of the north pier. The light stands twenty-five feet tall with an additional ten feet provided by the white cement foundation. A black lantern room adorns the top of the cast-iron tower. Many years ago there was a fog signal building connected to the light. A fourth-order Fresnel lens that once provided light has since been replaced by a modern red plastic beacon.

The pier and lighthouse were a focal point years ago for a ferry boat line traveling between Wisconsin and Michigan. Railroad cars were typically hauled via boat for many years at this location. The Menominee Lighthouse was automated in the early 1970s. Today, anglers frequent the pier in hopes of catching many Green Bay species.

When the nearby Green Island Light Station, five miles to the southeast, was automated in 1933, the Menominee Lighthouse took on added significance. Because the Menominee Light also featured an attended fog horn, it was the only remaining station in the area that could audibly warn seafarers in foggy conditions.

A United States Lighthouse Service keeper was stationed at the Menominee Lighthouse into the 1960s. Even though nearly all lighthouses were staffed by U.S. Coast Guard personnel by that time, the civilian keeper was in charge and was assisted by the Coast Guard.

39

40

Menominee North Pier Light

Ruins of the Green Island Lighthouse

What little remains of this once proud and valuable light lies in decay. Green Island, approximately ninety acres in size, is located in Green Bay, five miles southeast of the delta of the Menominee River and Marinette, Wisconsin. The ruins of the light lie on the far southeast end of the island. Underwater shoals extend from both the north and south ends of the island, making the island itself a navigational menace. The lighthouse was built in 1863 and the light first shone from a forty-foot-tall tower on October 1st of that year. The building was cream-colored brick with a cobblestone foundation. The light was originally fueled by lard oil and a fourth-order Fresnel lens emitted a fixed white light, visible for twelve miles.

Drew is a name closely linked to the history of Green Island. This family gave a significant portion of their lives, more than forty-one years, to service on the island. Samuel P. Drew was named Green Island's first keeper, holding this post until 1881. Mr. Drew began his tenure at Green Island Light with annual wages of $400. Four years later he was given a raise to $560. His wife, Mary, was named assistant keeper at this time and paid $400 annually. She held that post for three years. While stationed here the Drews made many improvements over and above those required for normal lighthouse maintenance. They constructed a pier to make it easier to dock and fish at the island, and a boathouse to protect their boat from the relentless wind and waves. They also farmed the island (one summer they sold eighty-seven bushels of strawberries) and kept a cow. Other structures and improvements included an outhouse, an oil storage house, a gasoline storage tank, sidewalks, a flagpole, and gardens. From all accounts, the Drews maintained an exceptionally clean lighthouse.

Sadly, the Drew family buried one of their children, Anna, who died at age three months, under a lilac bush near the lighthouse. Stormy weather prevented the Drews

Historic Green Island Light

courtesy Francis and Doris Cornell

41

from boating to the mainland to get medical attention for their child. On a happier note, two of the Drews' other daughters were married on Green Island. Their son, Frank, born in a bedroom under the Green Island Light, first became an assistant keeper here in 1903. He was promoted to keeper in 1909 and served the longest tenure of any keeper at Green Island, twenty years. He is credited with rescuing more than thirty people in several incidents around the island. Frank Drew also erected an array of mirrors to monitor the lantern beam from the snug comfort of the keepers quarters.

In 1864 a fire caused vast damage to the lighthouse and keeper's residence. Possibly caused by a kerosene explosion, the entire tower and lantern were severely damaged. A temporary light was built while major reconstruction was undertaken.

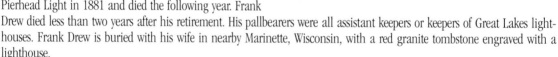

The Great Peshtigo Fire occurred in 1871, with smoke so thick that the Green Island Light was lit during the day to aid navigation. Mary Drew, a God-fearing person, sat at her kitchen table with her children and read from the Bible, believing the prophecy that the world was coming to a fiery end. All they could see in the distance were crimson flames while burning embers filled the air. Thick smoke from that fire was blamed for the wreck of the schooner *George Newman* on a reef at Green Island. The captain simply could not see the light beam through the smoke and became stranded on the reef.

Samuel Drew was transferred to the Menominee Pierhead Light in 1881 and died the following year. Frank Drew died less than two years after his retirement. His pallbearers were all assistant keepers or keepers of Great Lakes lighthouses. Frank Drew is buried with his wife in nearby Marinette, Wisconsin, with a red granite tombstone engraved with a lighthouse.

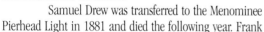

A Coast Guard Cutter, the USCGC Frank Drew, named in honor of the Green Island keeper, was christened and launched on December 5, 1998, at Marinette, Wisconsin.

Budget-cutting by the federal government doomed the Green Island Light. The last year that Green Island Light was manned was 1933. An automated acetylene gas lighting system was then installed. Slowly the noble lighthouse began to crumble from vandalism, lack of maintenance, and the elements. Later a second fire destroyed the brick tower. In the mid-1950s the Coast Guard constructed a sixty-foot tower topped with an automated battery-powered flashing light southeast of the original light. Currently the modern metal light tower is solar powered.

Today Green Island is overgrown with poison ivy, nettles, and thickets and lies abandoned. The future fate of the now almost exclusively privately owned island is unknown.

Current status: The lighthouse lies in ruins. A solar-powered light 65 feet tall on a metal pole flashes a white light every six seconds, with an 80-foot focal plane, visible for 10 miles. No fog signal.

How to get there: Accessible by boat only. Approximately five miles southeast of Marinette, Wisconsin. Local fishing guides may be hired to transport you out to the light.

*K*eeper James Wachter, a Native American, was keeper at Green Island Light from 1900 to 1909. His Native American wife smoked a corn-cob pipe. Native American burials are found in the center of the island.

⚓

43

Current light tower on Green Island

Peshtigo

Peshtigo is doubtless best known in Wisconsin history for the fiery hell that descended upon this small sawmill community on the evening of Sunday, October 8, 1871. The holocaust, known as the Great Peshtigo Fire, claimed eight hundred lives.

Another bit of Peshtigo's story, albeit considerably less well known, deals with the rocky ledge known as Peshtigo Reef that extends three miles out into Green Bay from Peshtigo Point. Treacherously shallow, with water depths of only one to six feet, the shoal has snared its share of vessels over the years.

Peshtigo Reef Lightship

Prior to the building of the lighthouse, the reef was guarded by Lightship No. 77, the *Peshtigo Reef Lightship*. Built in Michigan in 1905-1906 for approximately $14,000, this steel-hulled 155-ton vessel was 75 feet in length and almost 22 feet wide. Her ship number and the words "Peshtigo Reef" were painted in bold three-foot-tall white letters amidships on both sides of the vessel. The rear of the ship sported a wooden flag mast proudly displaying Old Glory. The lantern mast for the light was a steel tube that sported a daymarker when the light was not in use. Illuminating the lightship were a trio of oil-fueled lanterns. A metal fog signal bell was attached near the bow. The boat, lacking its own means of propulsion, had to be towed to its station.

The lightship was first placed on the reef on April 28, 1906, and stood guard seasonally. Typically her season began in March or April and ended in late November or early December. Wintertime lay-up in Sturgeon Bay was used for necessary repairs. August 26, 1935, was the lightship's final day on the reef. No longer needed because the Peshtigo Reef Lighthouse was placed into operation, the lightship's role changed to that of a relief light vessel. The boat was sold in 1940.

courtesy Bob Countillion, Peshtigo Historical Society

Peshtigo Reef Lightship

Peshtigo Reef Light

This modern, relatively new light was built in 1934 and stands seventy-two feet tall. A spherical cement crib base bordered by steel sheeting supports a metal tower. The station also contains a fog signal. A large red stripe divides the white tower, which helps to distinguish it out on the water. The light is operated automatically by a timer and solar panel. A stopping point for countless gulls and double-breasted cormorants, much of the foundation and tower are covered with whitewash.

Electronic innovations in the 1930s allowed this light and fog signal to be operated by radio remote control from the Sherwood Point Lighthouse in Door County, nine miles away, if its automatic clock mechanism failed or foggy conditions prevailed.

*P**rior to the use of navigational aids on Peshtigo Reef, the shoal routinely snared boats. A sailing vessel, the Wisconsin, ran aground in December, 1838, en route to Green Bay during a heavy gale and snowstorm. With frozen rigging and floating ice all around, the captain ordered his crew to disembark for fear that the large blocks of ice would crush the ship. In a letter of protest, Master John Beagie described being "driven upon the bar at (sic) Peshatico Point." Perhaps this event and many others convinced authorities to consider navigational help off this dangerous point.*

45

Current status: Active aid to navigation. White light flashes every six seconds, with a seventy-two-foot focal plane, visible for nine miles. Fog signal sounds a three-second blast in a thirty-second period. Peshtigo Reef Light is another beacon which the Coast Guard is interested in disposing of as excess property. Currently, options for the light are being explored. Being offshore adds difficulties to finding a permanent owner. Issues relating to drinking water and sewage disposal also need to be addressed.

How to get there: Accessible by boat only. Located three miles out in Green Bay. Local fish guides are a great resource to transport you out to the light. They will probably want you to go fishing, too!

Green Bay Harbor Entrance Light

"It's monotonous, boring . . . ."

—A Coast Guard crewman describing life in the early 1970s at the Green Bay Harbor Entrance Light.

This Brown County light was built in 1935 at the entrance to the Green Bay Harbor to replace several older beacons. Formerly known as Ten-Mile Light, this sentinel is slightly more than nine miles offshore from the city of Green Bay. Built on natural rock in about fifteen to twenty feet of water, Green Bay Harbor Entrance Light lies on the western edge of the primary shipping channel in lower Green Bay. The passage is dredged to keep larger vessels in a more concentrated area.

Coast Guard personnel, normally four men at a time, were stationed on this artificial island for two-week stays. The living quarters were a three-tiered complex. This was not a very spacious "home away from home" for those stationed here, and because this light was isolated, attempts were made to help personnel get along. However, there are stories of crewmen having some shouting matches and fistfights. These were generally short-lived, as there was no place for the men to go to "cool off" other than the bay! Reading, fishing, and card playing helped pass the time.

This light also took a pounding when the weather turned sour. Put yourself in the shoes of those stationed inside such a confining light during a Green Bay storm or when tempers flared.

This light is very similar in style and shape to the Peshtigo Reef Light. A circular concrete crib fifty feet in diameter forms the base. Safety was provided by chains, which circled the cement foundation. The white steel tower's focal plane is more than seventy feet above Green Bay. The lighthouse flashes a red light and houses a fog signal. A radio antenna also protrudes from the top of the tower.

During the boating season of its manned years, visitors would leave six-packs at the station. Beer was not prohibited on the light.

⚓

Current status: Active aid to navigation. Red occulting light from a fourth-order Fresnel lens flashes every four seconds, visible for twelve miles. A fog signal sounds a two second blast every fifteen seconds.

How to get there: Accessible only by boat. Located approximately nine miles off shore of Green Bay. The Green Bay Yacht Club may aid in arranging transportation to the light.

Green Bay Harbor Entrance Light

Ruins of the Long Tail Point Light

The massive stone tower that was the light at Long Tail Point was supposed to crumble decades ago. At the time of the shipping boom at the ports of Green Bay and De Pere on Green Bay, Long Tail Point was a sand spit, a slender sand bar island in the southernmost end of Green Bay. The island was detached from its peninsula by a canal, which was deep enough for fishing boats to use. The island and peninsula enveloped Dead Horse Bay. Fishermen utilized the bay for shelter and loggers used to store large log rafts here, destined for the Green Bay area sawmills. The Long Tail Point Light, about three and a quarter miles out in the bay, was placed to mark the entry into Green Bay and guide boats in and out of the mouth of the bay and the Fox River.

Long Tail Point is the oldest light in the region, established in 1847 and first lit in 1848, the same year Wisconsin achieved statehood. The lighthouse was built on footings in six feet of sand towards the southeast end of the island. When the tower boasted an iron lantern room, it stood more than eighty-five feet tall. It was built entirely of limestone, which was not quarried but picked up along the shore at Bay Settlement (across the bay on its eastern side) and brought across to the island by hand-

poled, hundred-foot scows. Stones of all shapes and sizes were employed. The only rocks that were quarried were the cap stones, just below the lantern. The tower is twenty-five feet in diameter at the base, with mammoth walls more than five feet thick. A keeper's residence, small in size, was built at this time but has long since disappeared. In 1859 the government deemed the lighthouse unsafe when high water lapped at the base. The wooden turret and lantern were removed, and the stone tower was considered an eyesore. A salvage contractor was hired but could not dismantle the mighty tower. The contractor soon gave up, quite disgusted, when the mortar tight rock would not be dislodged. Today, predictions of the light toppling into the water continue to persist. The "old stone tower" as it was called, has won this battle for decades. It stands as a monument to the early importance of the Green Bay area. We're hoping it survives for many more years.

In 1859 the original lantern room of the first lighthouse was placed on the peak of a new white-framed multi-story keeper's residence. This second lighthouse was known as Tail Point Light and was operated only during the shipping season. An old fog signal bell was replaced by a compressed air fog whistle. The new complex and the old tower were a favorite destination of excursion boats. A lovely sand beach and an outdoor terrace attracted many sightseers, picnickers, swimmers, and carolers. Because of the shallowness of the surrounding water, tourists were ferried to a pier that extended from the island. According to all accounts, the host at the lighthouse was "genial and courteous." It is no wonder that people were drawn to Long Tail Point.

Current status: In ruins. *Lighthouse Digest Magazine* lists the Long Tail Point Light on its "Doomsday List" of lights in danger of being lost forever.

How to get there: Located in Long Tail Point State Wildlife area, the lighthouse is accessible only by boat. The Green Bay Yacht Club is a possible resource to arrange transportation to the light. However there is no dock and you will experience a short but soggy walk to the light.

Grassy Island Front and Rear Range Lights

Grassy Island lies at the very southern end of Green Bay near the mouth of the Fox River. Merely a mile and a half from the river's mouth, originally the island blocked the main line entrance to the Green Bay harbor. Beginning in 1867 and ending several years later, Grassy Island underwent a dissection. A 650-foot long channel was dug straight through the low, wet island. The total path in the bay measured two hundred feet wide, nine feet deep, and was almost two miles long. Dredging continued annually to keep the basin navigable. Later the channel depth was increased.

The Grassy Island Range Lights, built in 1872, were located on an eastern embankment that was cut through the island, enabling seamen to recognize the deepened artificial navigation channel in lower Green Bay. The Grassy Island Range Lights were of a fixed white character for many years until they were changed in 1934 to a flashing green color to enable them to stand out from the background of Green Bay's city lights.

The Grassy Island complex was a well-maintained and interesting site. Many structures stood on this small island, including a separate two-and-a-half-story keeper's dwelling with an attached porch, a flagpole, boathouse, pier, and two range lights—the taller upper (rear) light and the smaller lower (front) light. Both lights were wooden pyramid shaped structures, painted white. The taller and slightly more slender rear light, which was closer to the mouth of the Fox River, stood at a height of approximately thirty-five feet. The shorter, slightly more stout front range light was nearly twenty-five feet tall. Both lights

Grassy Island Front Range Light

49

were topped with an eight-sided lantern room and a metal walkway near the top of each tower. Both lights had a doorway at ground level for the keeper. The lights were positioned several hundred feet apart, along an all-wooden pier consisting of railroad tie-type planks. These wooden range lights formed a north-south line to guide boats within the navigable channel of Green Bay.

In this situation the range lights indicated a channel centerline. The front light is the lower of the two and nearer the mariner. The rear light is the higher of the two and is further from

In the 1880s, Green Bay was the largest flour-shipping port on the Great Lakes.

⚓

Grassy Island Rear Range Light

the mariner, who positioned the two lights, one above the other, to locate the centerline.

The lights remained in service until 1966, at which time it was suggested that they be burned so that additional dredging of the harbor could be undertaken. Another portion of the island was excavated and removed during the additional dredging. Progressive thinking members of the Green Bay Yacht Club rescued the wooden lights from certain destruction and brought them to the Yacht Club by barge. They were later moved to land by crane with the assistance of the U.S. Coast Guard.

Recently, a project was undertaken by Yacht Club members to move the lights to their permanent home at the club, to position them as range lights, and to restore them. As of this writing, both lights have been permanently moved to their sheet pile bases. The Grassy Island Range Lights exterior will then be restored and lights will be placed back in both towers. At their new home, the Grassy Island Range Lights will be a reminder of their valuable function of years ago.

Current Grassy Island Range Lights

Current status: Inactive; being restored by the private Green Bay Yacht Club on club grounds. Currently, wooden shingles and siding cover both lighthouses.

How to get there: In Green Bay, take I-43 to exit #187 (Webster Ave.). At the first stop sign turn right. Go one block to a 4-way stop sign at N. Irwin Ave. Turn left (north) onto Irwin, which becomes Bay Beach Road. Follow this past Bay Beach Park for approximately one mile. Watch for the sign "Green Bay Metro Boat Landing" on your left. Turn left and park in the public parking lot near the Yacht Club.

52

Cana Island Lighthouse

Door County.

Steadfast, serene, immovable, the same
Year after year, through all the silent night
Burns on forevermore that quenchless flame,
Shines on that inextinguishable light!

—from "The Lighthouse", by Henry Wadsworth Longfellow

Cave Point

Door County, Wisconsin's "thumb" extending into Lake Michigan, is notable for many things beyond its uniquely beautiful landscape. Bordered by the sometimes treacherous waters of Lake Michigan on the east and Green Bay to the west, the name is derived from "Door to Death," as the Native Americans called it, and Porte des Morte (Death's Door) as it was known to the first French fur traders. The narrow, six-mile-wide strait between the tip of the peninsula and Washington Island connecting the waters of the lake and the bay has violent currents at times, dangerous shoals and reefs, and two small islands in it. Powerful and capricious shifting winds off Lake Michigan also play a part in the unpredictability of the strait. Many factual stories confirm the Door's legend of death. For example, in 1872 more than a hundred large craft were stranded or damaged while trying to navigate Death's Door. In 1880 at least thirty boats were driven ashore on Plum Island.

Part of the rocky Niagara escarpment, which extends from New York State's natural wonder, Niagara Falls, to Iowa, the Door peninsula is approximately seventy miles in length. Consisting of resistant Silurian limestone and dolomite cliffs and embankments, Door County is rugged and unrivaled in a variety of ways. Sometimes called the "Cape Cod of the Midwest," it boasts more lighthouses (10), more miles of shoreline (250), and more state parks (5), than any county in the contiguous United States! The lighthouses played a crucial part of its nautical history as Door County became a hub of maritime commerce. Despite the presence of lighthouses, however, scores of ships still perished in the waters surrounding the peninsula.

Annually the Door County Maritime Museum sponsors a Lighthouse Walk in mid-May. Presently, nine of the lighthouses are open to the public, with historical information provided. Combinations of walking tours, boat trips, and special touring opportunities make for an exciting weekend for the lighthouse buff. Contact the Door County Maritime Museum, (920) 743-5958, or the Door County Chamber of Commerce, (920) 743-4456, for additional information.

The Museum has two locations: One is in Sturgeon Bay at 120 N. Madison Ave., (920)-743-5958; open Memorial Day through Labor Day daily 9-6, Labor Day to Memorial Day daily 10-5. This location features a new 20,000-square-foot year-round building housing an excellent Great Lakes model ship exhibit, interactive exhibits, lighthouse artwork, and much more. The second location is in Memorial Park at Gills Rock. (920)-854-1844; open Memorial Day-Labor Day daily 10-4, Sunday 1-4; September through mid-October, daily 12-4, Sunday 1-4. It features commercial fishing, shipwreck, navigation and lifesaving exhibits.

At present, certain lighthouses of Door County continue to play a meaningful role as aids to navigation. Today the faithful keepers are gone and the lights are automated. With this change, some of these historic structures have deteriorated. Human intervention will be necessary to arrest this trend, otherwise their demise may be irreversible.

Recently the U. S. Coast Guard has determined that several Door County lighthouses are no longer necessary for maritime safety and is planning to "dispose" of the properties. The future long term stewardship, ownership, and management of Eagle Bluff, Pilot Island, Plum Island, and Cana Island lighthouses is currently under discussion. The Bureau of Land Management, an agency of the U.S. Department of the Interior, is coordinating the disposition of these lights and is soliciting citizen input. The lights are in need of various degrees of restoration. As diverse as the lighthouses themselves are the opinions concerning the beacons' future. Private or public ownership, acquisition as State Park land, conversion to nautical historic museums, and many other ideas are all possible end uses of these magnificent and historically significant beacons. Have you ever thought of "adopting" a lighthouse? You might get the chance.

Sherwood Point Lighthouse

Named for Peter Sherwood, who settled on the Point in 1836, a finger-like projection of land overlooks the confluence of the western and southern end of Sturgeon Bay into Green Bay. A lighthouse was built here in 1883, in response to the opening of the Sturgeon Bay Shipping Canal which increased maritime traffic many fold. When the city of Sturgeon Bay was scarcely seven years old, a light was needed to guide vessels traveling from the west on Green Bay into Sturgeon Bay and to steer schooners and steamships around reefs and shoals. Construction materials used to build the light station arrived by boat and were hauled up the steep bank. The tower is thirty-five feet tall and sits atop a limestone bluff, part of which had to be dynamited to build the foundation for the lighthouse. The light's total height above Green Bay is sixty feet. A stone fence separates the 1.1 acres of government-owned grounds from the bluff and bay.

Sherwood Point is a unique Door County light. It is the lone lighthouse in the county constructed of red brick and resembles an old red schoolhouse. The original light was first lit on October 10, 1883, and exhibited a white color that alternated with red flashes of one-minute intervals. Mineral oil was the original fuel. Because mechanical problems with the light's clockwork mechanism caused it to break down frequently, it was replaced in the early 1890s with a fourth-order Fresnel lens which remains in

In 1884 Minnie Hesh, of Brooklyn, New York, visited Door County and enjoyed it so much that she moved there. Sometime later she married William Cochems who was to become the assistant keeper at Sherwood Point. When Cochems was named keeper, Minnie was designated assistant keeper. She remained in that capacity until her death in 1928. Today there is a plaque to honor Minnie in the form of a stone with her name inscribed upon it. The stone rests in a small stone planter east of the keeper's quarters.

55

Sherwood Point Lighthouse

operation today. A separate white pyramid-shaped wooden fog signal building was also built that year and still stands in front of the lighthouse. Originally, a bell rang several times a minute to alert mariners in the area during foggy conditions. Compressed air foghorns, whose moan could be heard for ten miles, eventually replaced the bell. A summer kitchen with a sloping roof was added to the back of the house. A fuel-storage building also survives and is made of red brick with a red roof. Steps lead down from the light to the water and an old concrete pier juts into the bay.

The first keeper was Henry Stanley, who was transferred from the Eagle Bluff Lighthouse. The station opened as early as March or as late as May, depending on ice conditions in the bay. Stanley and his family lived a rugged existence. Indoor plumbing would not be installed at Sherwood Point until 1945. Stanley hunted in the woods to supplement the chickens and cows the family raised along with vegetables and fruit from their garden.

Henry Stanley's death allowed William Cochems to be promoted from assistant to head lightkeeper. Minnie Cochems, William's wife, and niece of Henry Stanley, was an assistant keeper at Sherwood Point for three decades.

Sherwood Point Lighthouse also holds the distinction and prestige of being the final manned light on the Great Lakes. Ironically, after celebrating its centennial, the light was automated. To insure that the light never goes out, a six-bulb lamp changer, resembling a Ferris wheel, is in operation. When one bulb burns out the mechanism rotates and the next light turns on. On August 27, 1983, an era ended in both Wisconsin and the Great Lakes when Sherwood Point Lighthouse no longer had a human presence.

Current status: Active aid to navigation. A white isophase light from a fourth-order Fresnel lens cycles three seconds on and three seconds off, visible for sixteen miles. The fog signal building is no longer in use, the foghorn having been moved to a buoy, a mile offshore. An old radio beacon has been discontinued as well. The lighthouse quarters are utilized by the Coast Guard for rest and recreation. The grounds are private and the light and building are not open to the public. During the annual Door County Lighthouse Walk in May, the grounds may be toured.

How to get there: Located west of Sturgeon Bay, north of Potawatomi State Park. PRIVATE.

Chambers Island Lighthouse

Chambers Island is located midway between Wisconsin and Michigan in the waters of Green Bay, nearly six miles northwest of Peninsula State Park. The lighthouse is located on the northwest shore of the island. Colonel Talbot Chambers, for whom the island is named, began an army post at the headwaters of Green Bay and was the leader of the expedition that named Washington Island. Chambers Island is three miles long and one and a half miles wide, the largest island within Green Bay and the second largest in Door County. Early island activities included building ships, fishing, and lumbering.

This Cream City brick story-and-a-half structure was built in 1868 for less than ten thousand dollars to mark the treacherous shoals around the island and mark the western shipping channel of Green Bay. The tower is forty-two feet tall, the lower half square and the upper portion eight-sided. A fourth-order Fresnel lens, lit for the first time in the autumn of 1868, displayed a steady white light that flashed twice a minute through the ten-sided lantern room.

Built the same year as its twin sister at Eagle Bluff, the keeper's quarters are also identical. The only difference is between the two light towers. The one at Chambers Island is octagonal; while that of Eagle Bluff is square and is set into the house diagonally. The towers were designed this way intentionally so that during daytime hours sailors would be able to distinguish each lighthouse from the other and know their position on the bay.

The first Chambers Island keeper was Lewis Williams, who had previously owned this location and operated a sawmill on the island. With his wife Anna they raised eleven children. Williams served here for more than two decades, the longest of any of the nine keepers who tended this lighthouse. It is hard to imagine thirteen people in the small lighthouse building. The light was manned full-time by civilian keepers until the Coast Guard assumed control during World War II.

Chambers Island Light was first automated in 1955 when a thirty-foot tower was erected where

Years ago a rumor persisted that a stolen payroll from Fort Howard was buried somewhere on Chambers Island.

⚓

the former lens room stood. A new and higher metal tower with daymarker symbols was put into service with a battery-powered light in 1961. This light tower stands closer to the water and is separate from the old lighthouse. Today, the light is solar-powered.

Listed on the National Register of Historical Buildings, Chambers Island Lighthouse became a forty-acre Town of Gibraltar Day Park in 1976. Named Chambers Island Lighthouse Town Park, picnickers are welcome. Caretakers have been responsible for the lighthouse's upkeep for more than two decades. When they are in residence you can still climb the fifty-four steps from the basement to the top of the tower. Opening the hatch at the top affords a grand view of the grounds and the bay.

Today the lighthouse remains, minus its lantern room. The original lantern room and Fresnel lens are currently part of a collection in Pioneer Village, located in Minden, Nebraska. The former keeper's office at the lighthouse is now a "history room" containing Chambers Island and lighthouse historic materials.

Current status: Inactive. A 67-foot modern metal tower beacon separate from the lighthouse flashes a white light every 6 seconds, visible for 10 miles. No fog signal.

How to get there: Limited access by excursion boat. Contact Joel and Mary Ann Blahnik, 9171 Spring Rd, Fish Creek, WI 54212, (920) 868-3100, who have been Chambers Island Lighthouse caretakers ever since the property was turned over to the Town of Gibraltar.

Eagle Bluff Lighthouse

This historic light marks the eastern passage into Green Bay from Lake Michigan and guards the shallow Strawberry Channel. Built in 1868, the same year as its sister lighthouse at Chambers Island, the Eagle Bluff Lighthouse was also constructed of Cream City brick. On a five-story limestone bluff overlooking the bay of Green Bay, the square tower and ten-sided lantern room stand forty-three feet tall. Along with the tower and main living room, the house boasts a kitchen, several bedrooms, and a sitting room. Green shutters grace the windows of the main house. Eagle Bluff Light is located in Peninsula State Park, Wisconsin's largest park and one of its most popular, with nearly 3,800 acres nestled between Fish Creek and Ephraim in an area formerly called Lighthouse Bay. Originally a fixed white light produced from a three-and-a-half-order Fresnel lens that was oil-fueled could be seen over the Green Bay for sixteen miles. This was replaced in 1918 by a fifth-order Fresnel lens.

Only three keepers called Eagle Bluff Light home. The first was Henry Stanley, whose tenure lasted a decade and a half. He was later transferred to the light at Sherwood Point. Much of the historical record of the Eagle Bluff Light, however, is a biography of the Duclon family. William Duclon, Eagle Light's second keeper, served for thirty-five years. Mr. Duclon and his wife Julia raised seven children, all boys, at the lighthouse. Duclon earned thirty dollars a month, plus supplies. This was considered an excellent wage in the late 1800s. Since supplies were brought to this post only once a year, by boat, the Duclon family supplemented their rations with a vegetable garden. Meat was procured by hunting in the nearby woods. The Duclon family also kept cows and chickens for fresh milk and eggs. Water was carried up from the lake via wooden steps until a well was drilled and a horse walking on a treadmill provided the power to bring up the water. The Commodore inspected the light station on an annual basis and the Duclons were given several commendations for "the best looking lighthouse grounds in the Great Lakes area."

Eagle Bluff Light was extinguished at the end of the sailing season, usually December or January, and the keeper was then allowed to take a few days off! Being a nearly self-sufficient family, the Duclons nearest medical help was in the city of Green Bay, nearly sixty miles to the south by boat and almost seventy miles over a very poor road system. The modern comforts of electricity and indoor plumbing were never installed at Eagle Bluff. This is still true today! William and Julia Duclon are buried in Blossemberg Cemetery in Peninsula State Park.

Eagle Bluff Lighthouse

Because the light tower was the highest point on the bluff, it was often struck by lightning. The lightning would travel down the circular, iron staircase of the tower, damaging walls and furnishings on its way.

Eagle Bluff Lighthouse was manned until 1926 when it became automated. It remained vacant until the middle 1930s when the State of Wisconsin leased it as part of its park system. The lighthouse had fallen on hard times between its automation and the time it was given a new lease on life by the Door County Historical Society. Before the keeper's quarters were restored, eighty layers of gray paint were removed from the interior walls, floors, ceilings, and woodwork. In the 1800s, paint came in a rectangular can as a powder, which was mixed with water. When any one of the seven Duclon boys got into trouble, their parents handed them a brush and told them to paint. It is safe to say that they must have been in a lot of trouble!

The Eagle Bluff Lighthouse has been turned into a museum. Restored and furnished by the Door County Historical Society, Eagle Bluff appears as it would have in the late 1800s when the Duclon family was in residence. Guided informational tours are conducted daily from 10 a.m. until 4:30 p.m., June through mid-October. A modest admission fee is charged. One of the best of only a handful of guided lighthouse tours in Wisconsin, visitors are offered a glimpse into a bygone era. You may still climb the circular iron steps of the tower to just below the level of the Fresnel lens. The keeper's dwelling has been completely restored with many original artifacts on display. The Eagle Bluff restoration began in 1960 with tours commencing in 1964. The Duclons would be proud of the way their light has been preserved for future generations.

The complex also contains two small out buildings of Cream City brick, one an outhouse, the other a fuel storage building. An old ship's anchor weighing half a ton is also on display on the lighthouse grounds. It was taken from the schooner *Oak Leaf*, which was launched April 14, 1866, and sank in Sturgeon Bay sixty years later.

Current status: Active aid to navigation and museum. The old fifth-order Fresnel lens at Eagle Bluff Light is still positioned in its tower but is non-functional. A modern solar-powered light atop the tower outside the lantern room now performs this task. The white light flashes every six seconds and is visible for seven miles. No fog signal. The U.S. Coast Guard has declared this historic light unnecessary for maritime safety. It is hoped that the Door County Historical Society will continue its marvelous maintenance of the light. Eagle Bluff Lighthouse is listed on the National Register of Historic Places. Contact Wayne and Ruby Lemburg, 7698 W. Kangaroo Lake Dr., Baileys Harbor, WI 54202, or the Door County Historical Society.

How to get there: Located in Peninsula State Park, between Fish Creek and Ephraim on Hwy. 42. All visitors must pay the daily park admission fee or have a current annual park sticker. A map of the park may be obtained at the park entrance.

Pottawatomie Lighthouse on Rock Island

The original Pottawatomie Light of 1836 was the oldest of all Wisconsin lighthouses, the first federal government lighthouse in Wisconsin on Lake Michigan. To put this date in perspective, 1836 was the year that Wisconsin became a territory, still a dozen years before statehood. Andrew Jackson was President. The 1871 Peshtigo fire still was 35 years in the future.

Rock Island is probably the place French explorer Robert LaSalle visited in 1679. LaSalle did a brisk fur trade with the Native Americans in this area. He had a boat built, the *Griffon*, to transport the furs economically and quickly. On

60

An Inspector from the Lighthouse Service met with keeper Corbin in 1845. The inspector reported that Corbin was most competent but lonely, his only company being his dog and a horse. Corbin was given three weeks of rest and recuperation with the stipulation that he bring back a wife! He did not succeed. Corbin died at his station and is interred in a small graveyard not far from his beloved light.

September 2, 1679, the cargo ship left Mackinac, arriving at Washington Island's Detroit Harbor several days later. After the ship was laden with pelts, the *Griffon* left port on September 18th. She was on her way home and was never heard from again. The *Griffon* not only had the distinction of being the first sailing vessel on the Great Lakes, but was also the first unexplained shipwreck on the Great Lakes.

Pottawatomie Light is named after Rock Island's early Native American inhabitants. The name appropriately means "Keeper of the Fire." Rock Island sits northeast of Door County's largest isle, Washington Island. The lighthouse is perched on the northwest end of the 900-plus-acre island, 137 feet atop sheer limestone on a bluff called Potawatomi Point. Because of the island's strategic location, where Green Bay and Lake Michigan converge, a significant merchant shipping lane existed here in what was termed the Rock Island Passage, the gateway between the two bodies of water. Rock Island was an important stepping stone between the Straits of Mackinac and regions south, including Green Bay and the Fox River leading to the Mississippi Valley. The shipping season ran from approximately the beginning of April through mid-December. Rock Island is Wisconsin's most northeastern point and separates Wisconsin's Door County from Michigan's Garden peninsula and nearby islands. Rock Island is believed to be the first place in Wisconsin visited by Europeans. The earliest European settlement in Door County was here. The island served fishermen and trappers and functioned as a trading post.

David E. Corbin had the distinction of being Pottawatomie's and Wisconsin's first light keeper, serving until his death in 1852. A sergeant during the War of 1812, Corbin became one of the first non-Native American settlers on Rock Island.

Built before Fresnel lens technology was implemented, the original watchful light contained a Winslow Lewis lamp in its eight-sided lantern room. The apparatus was complete with reflectors and was oil-fueled. In 1858 the thirty-foot stone lighthouse and keeper's quarters were demolished and the dolomite lighthouse seen today was built. Faulty grout was used in the first lighthouse and the building was marred by moisture damage. The new forty-one-foot tower utilized a fourth-order Fresnel lens with a fixed white light that could be seen for sixteen miles. Old photos record the lighthouse area with virtually no trees surrounding it and a white board fence at the edge of the cliffs. Other buildings in the lighthouse complex included an outhouse, a barn, a chicken coop, and an oil storage house. Today, the oil storage building remains. A garden and fruit trees were also on the grounds. One account also documents the basement of the lighthouse being used as a schoolhouse for local children. Several children could also call Pottawatomie Lighthouse their birthplace.

Pottawatomie Light was automated in 1946. Later the nine-sided lantern room in the tower was dismantled, the Fresnel lens was removed, and a small battery-powered beacon-type light was installed atop the house. It was replaced in the 1980s by a separate forty-one-foot metal tower west of the lighthouse that was solar-powered. What became of the lantern room and the Fresnel lens that was stolen from storage many years ago is still a mystery.

Current status: Pottawatomie Lighthouse is in the process of being restored. The Friends of Rock Island (FORI), a non-profit organization, has implemented a multi-year restoration and refurbishing plan. In June of 1999 the first phase was completed. A new nine-sided, copper-roofed lantern room was placed atop the tower. Supporters of the project described the placing of the ventilator ball atop the lantern room as similar to "putting the cherry on a sundae." Later, after restoration of the interior of the keeper's quarters is completed, the Friends expect interpretive tours of the lighthouse to begin in the summer of 2002. Plans call for a volunteer guide living on site for public tours and, with DNR approval, the furnishing of two rooms for overnight rental. Additional interior work on the keeper's quarters will continue as well. The Friends are optimistic that one day a light will again adorn the new lantern room. For further information contact the Friends of Rock Island, 126 Country Club Dr., Clintonville, WI 54929. Send e-mail to cmarlspc@uniontel.net. Visit the FORI web site at www.wctc.net/~cmarlspc

Today a square, modern metal tower with a beacon, located near the old lighthouse, sends out a warning to mariners. The white light flashes every four seconds, visible for seven miles, with a 159-foot focal plane, one of the higher ones on the Great Lakes. No fog signal.

How to get there: Pottawatomie Light is one of the more challenging Wisconsin lights to reach. A car ferry from either Gills Rock or Northport to Washington Island is required to get to Pottawatomie. The boat docks at the south end of Washington Island. Then make your way by car, bike, moped, or taxi to the north end of Washington Island to Jackson Harbor, where you will take the Rock Island (Karfi) ferry to the island. There is no direct ferry service to Rock Island from the Door mainland. Once on Rock Island, you hike approximately 1.25 miles to the lighthouse over an uphill, rooted, rocky, and at times forested path, which levels off and then continues downhill to the lighthouse. There was evidence of poison ivy when we visited, so remain on the path. Currently, occasional tours are held and the lighthouse is then open. If you are fortunate enough to make the climb to the lantern room, you will be rewarded with a spectacular view of Lake Michigan and Green Bay. There are 73 steps that lead down to the rocky beach below the lighthouse, where you can view the majestic limestone bluffs. No food is sold on the island, so it's a good idea to pack a lunch to carry in. Rock Island is a Wisconsin State Park, currently uninhabited except for the park ranger. Camping and hiking are allowed but no vehicles, including bicycles, are permitted on the island.

Plum Island Range Lights

"Plumb" in the middle of the treacherous Death's Door passage (it is not known precisely when the "b" was dropped), Plum Island sits where Lake Michigan links Green Bay, between the end of the main Door peninsula and Washington Island.

The original Plum Island Lighthouse was built in 1848 but was moved to Pilot Island some years later. The Plum Island Range Lights were constructed in 1896 and first lit the following year. The lights are located on the southern end of the island, the Front Light to the east, the Rear Range Light about a third of a mile to the west. These lights guide sailors safely from Lake Michigan through this sometimes difficult passage into Green Bay. The Rear Range Light consists of a tubular and skeletal shaped tower sixty-five feet tall capped with a red lantern top and ventilator ball that houses a fourth-order Fresnel lens with a fixed red beam. A spacious two-story keeper's dwelling and a fog signal building stand nearby. The original Front Range Light was a wooden tower and was close to the beach on the island's southeast shore. It harbored a smaller sixth-order Fresnel lens with a steady red color. A modern, metal skeletal forty-foot tower took its place in the mid-1960s. The Range Lights were automated in 1969. The current Range Lights sport a banner with red stripes on either side of a middle white stripe to serve as a daymarker. There are stairs leading to the top of the front (lower) range light. When the Plum

Plum Island Front Range Light

63

Island lights were manned there was a pier that extended out into the bay, a tram for transporting supplies, and a boathouse. Other structures on the lighthouse grounds include a white building to the west of the rear range lighthouse where the fog signal resided.

Plum Island also was home to a lifesaving station on the northern side of the island. The attached tower was not a lighthouse, but a "lookout station." From the mid- to late 1800s dozens of lifesaving stations were frequently placed in areas with an above-average number of shipwrecks on the Great Lakes. The Death's Door area certainly qualified for that distinction. The lifesaving station here was responsible for many rescues. Later the facility was converted into a Coast Guard Station. It was abandoned and relocated to Washington Island in the early 1990s. The old station is currently in a state of decay.

Martin Knudsen was the first keeper of these range lights, beginning in 1897. By the time of his retirement, he had served a total of forty-four years, including stints at Pilot Island in Door County and North Point Lighthouse in Milwaukee.

Plum Island Rear Range Light

Current status: Active aids to navigation. The rear range light displays a fixed, red light from a fourth-order Fresnel lens. The front range light is a red isophase light that cycles three seconds on and three seconds off. Today the island is overgrown. Walkways that led to the fog signal building and Lower Range Light are lichen-covered, disintegrating pieces of concrete. The former keeper's building has boarded-up windows and is in a general state of disrepair. The Coast Guard Auxiliary re-roofed the dwelling in the summer of 1999. The Coast Guard considers the Plum Island lights surplus property. There are discussions that the State of Wisconsin might take over the island as a possible new State park. Non-profit or "friends" groups are another option for halting Plum Island's slow decline. Repair and renovation costs here would be significant.

How to get there: Plum Island is owned by the federal government and maintained by the U.S. Coast Guard. It is currently closed to the public, but during the Annual Door County Lighthouse Walk held during mid-May each year, those interested in lighthouses have been able to land here. From the abandoned Coast Guard Life Saving Station and dock on the north side of the island you can hike the approximately 0.6 mile trail to view the range lights. Contact the Door County Chamber of Commerce, (920) 743-4456. At other times you can take the car ferry from either Gills Rock or Northport and cruise past the island. Sightseeing boat tours from Gills Rock go past Plum Island for viewing and photography on their way to Washington Island.

Pilot Island Lighthouse

Pilot Island and its lighthouse have, without a doubt, seen better days. The light station and island no longer are the vibrant place they once were. Best described as three and a half acres of rocks, Pilot Island is located east of Northport at the tip of the Door peninsula, approximately two miles from an area known as the Porte des Morts or Death's Door. This area is particularly dangerous with numerous shoals to the south. Strategically located on the eastern edge of the Door passage, the landmark Pilot Island received its name because it was used by early sailors as a "pilot" to navigate this tricky passage. Early in its history the lighthouse was known as Port des Morts Light Station.

The legend of the station is one of loneliness, numerous shipwrecks, dramatic rescues, and drownings. The desolation of this, one of the loneliest light stations, may have contributed to the suicide of assistant keeper John Boyce in the summer of 1880. Another report states that Pilot Island holds the record for witnessing the most shipwrecks of any Great Lakes lighthouse. During the early 1870s, for example, the lighthouse keeper's diary recorded over a hundred ships lost or damaged in this treacherous strait. While stationed here, keepers were credited with saving several lives. The sailing ships of days gone by were much more vulnerable than today's motorized vessels. Despite a light here, Death's Door more than lived up to its name.

The first light station in this strait was actually built in 1848 on Plum Island, two miles to the west, and later re-built on Pilot Island. It was determined that a more easterly light was needed. In 1858 a two-story Cream City brick residence was built with a thirty-seven-foot-tall tower. Undersized when the light was relocated on Pilot Island, the height of the original tower was increased to forty-six feet, and a fourth-order Fresnel lens focused the light. In its heyday the Pilot Island Lighthouse complex also included a pier, barn, a foghorn building, and outhouse.

Fog enveloped Pilot Island for dozens of days during the shipping season. The fog signal was quite a thunderous contraption, the

Pilot Island Light, 1955

courtesy Jack A. Eckert

65

loudest on the Great Lakes. It could be heard for more than twelve miles. Driven by compressed air, the monotonous two-tone sound would be activated in foggy conditions and was deafening. The foghorn roar on Pilot Island was so terrible, the eggs laid by the chickens would never hatch!

When the Coast Guard operated this station, a minimum of two men were required for duty. The shipping season typically began the last week of March and ran through October. Accounts record a tremendous amount of hard work needed to keep the station in top shape. Despite the toil and thunderous fog signal, however, Pilot Island could be a peaceful place.

Power for the lighthouse in the middle 1950s was provided by a group of batteries powered by twin generators. Propane fueled a stove and refrigerator. At times, an item of relative luxury, a television, was also available.

The U.S. Coast Guard abandoned this facility in 1962 when it was automated. Slowly the old lighthouse fell into a state of disrepair. Today the boarded-up keeper's quarters and fog signal building are merely the bony remains of how things used to be. Several years ago, however, a group of Coast Guard personnel repaired the leaking and dilapidated roof to help stabilize the house. Twice a year the facility and light get a maintenance check from the Coast Guard. Hundreds of cormorants and seagulls have taken over the island and the stench from their waste is said to be so strong that a gas mask

Pilot Island Lighthouse

would be necessary to keep a person from being overcome. Most of the trees on Pilot Island have died as a result of the massive amount of avian droppings.

Current status: Active aid to navigation. Pilot Island light has a distinct flash pattern and is termed an eclipsing light. In a six-second period the light flashes for one second, goes dark for another second, flashes again for one second, and is dark for three seconds. A modern plastic lens now sends its light out across Death's Door. Visible for 12 miles. The lantern room exterior is equipped with solar panels and a radio antenna. The island is owned by the federal government and maintained by the U.S. Coast Guard. The lighthouse is closed to the public.

Pilot Island Lighthouse is currently listed by the Coast Guard as excess property. It is one of several Door County lights where long-term ownership is being sought. Pilot Island and its lighthouse are in dire need of significant rehabilitation. This is one lighthouse that will require a serious commitment if it is to survive.

How to get there: You can take the car ferry from either Gills Rock or Northport. These cruise past the island for viewing and photography, but do not stop there. During the Annual Door County Lighthouse Walk, cruise ships will pass by the island and stop for viewing and photography.

Cana Island Lighthouse

A visit to Cana Island Lighthouse is a journey back through time. An integral part of the peninsula's history, this beacon is a titan among Wisconsin lights, the most distinctive of Door County's scenic landmarks and one of its greatest tourist attractions. A photographer's and artist's delight, this historic light has guided ships and sailors around the island's rugged shoreline for more than 130 years. It has witnessed ferocious storms and the subsequent demise of many ships along the shallow, treacherous reefs. The keepers' logs tell graphic tales of violent storms, especially in the 1870s when Lake Michigan's water level was abnormally high. One storm destroyed seven ships near the island; huge waves broke over the house and spray reached the lantern room and glass near the top of the tower! Daring rescues and the drudgery of everyday life on the island are also a part of the written history of the light.

During the winter of 1877, the lighthouse keeper, William Sanderson, spotted a small boat embedded in an ice floe off Cana Island. Two human figures, a father and son, sat hunched over in the vessel. Frozen to death, they drifted past the lighthouse and were never seen again.

The U.S. Lighthouse Service chose Cana Island because it was strategically located between two good natural harbors, North Bay and Moonlight Bay, where ships in jeopardy could find refuge before encountering the Death's Door passage to the north.

If you visit only one lighthouse in Wisconsin, this striking sentinel is highly recommended. If you picture in your mind what a lighthouse should look like, Cana Island Light fits the image. No other Door County beacon looks like it. Originally a footbridge connected the island to the shoreline. A dock and boathouse also were located south of the present causeway. Today the trek across the five-hundred-foot-long limestone causeway from the mainland to the nearly nine-acre dolomite island is well worth getting your feet (and sometimes more) wet. The water level can vary from bone dry to nearly thigh-deep, depending on lake level. The lighthouse is located on the easternmost point of the rocky island, down a meandering trail where years ago horse and buggy trod. Today thimbleberries line the path in the summertime. Limestone walls built by one of the keepers in the 1920s can also be seen on the lighthouse grounds near the tower.

Built in 1869 and first lit early in 1870, the white tower stands eighty-six feet tall, with a spiral staircase of ninety-eight steps and a focal plane of eighty-nine feet above lake level. The tower walls are massive, nearly four feet thick at the base. It was originally constructed of the same yellowish Milwaukee Cream City brick as the house, but was covered with fifteen tiers of riveted iron sheeting early in the twentieth century to prevent weathering of the brickwork. The house and light tower were the first buildings constructed on the island. At the time of construction it was the tallest building in Door County, spacious enough to accommodate two households. Numerous families lived here, serving as keepers, assistants, and caretakers. Children were born and raised on Cana Island. Poignant island memories include wedding celebrations and weeping when beloved family members' ashes were strewn on the island.

Power for the light changed with the years and advancing technology. The first fuel was lard oil, burned in a lamp with a wick. Other fuels included whale oil, kerosene, acetylene, and an explosive naphtha formula. Eventually the light was converted to electricity, first from batteries and later from a generator. The power lines you see today date to the 1960s. Cana Island Lighthouse still has no running water and the bathroom facilities are outdoors.

The original third-order Fresnel lens, nearly five feet tall, is still in operation today. Its light is visible for approximately seventeen miles over Lake Michigan. The light was automated in 1944 and is currently illuminated by a small projection bulb. Four rotating, automatically changeable bulbs prevent the light from going dark for more than an instant.

The Cana Island Lighthouse is presently under the jurisdiction of the U.S. Coast Guard, which still operates it. Maintenance is performed by the Aids to Navigation Team from Green Bay. Louis and Rosie Janda and family served as caretakers, residing at the lighthouse during the summer months for nearly two decades before the light station lost its human presence in the autumn of 1995. The grounds are open daily from mid-May through October, but the tower is not open to the public. Now a National Historic Site, the lighthouse has been licensed for more than a quarter of a century to the Door County Maritime Museum, Inc., which assisted in its renovation. The keeper's quarters may be toured when Museum staff are on duty. The Museum's philosophy is to continue to keep the island as it once was, so all can enjoy its historic ambience. Cana Island continues to occupy a natural setting, far removed from the hustle and bustle of the peninsula, letting you easily imagine life on the island as it was a century ago.

Cana Island Lighthouse

Current status: Active aid to navigation. The fixed white light, provided by a 500-watt bulb projected through the original third-order Fresnel lens, is visible for 17 miles. Cana Island's future is in the hands of the federal government. The keeper's house, while not restored, is open when Museum personnel are on duty. The tower is not accessible because the light is still in service. For further information, contact the Door County Maritime Museum, 120 N. Madison Ave., PO Box 246, Sturgeon Bay, WI 54235. Telephone (920) 743-5958 or e-mail at dcmm@itol.com

Changes continue to unfold on Cana Island. The lighthouse is one of several Door County lights declared excess property by the U.S. government. Finding a permanent owner who will insure the future of the light will be, it is hoped, the next stage in this magnificent beacon's long and storied history.

How to get there: From Baileys Harbor, go north on Hwy. 57. Turn right (east) at County Q. Continue past Moonlight Bay. Watch for Cana Island sign at approximately 3.5 miles and turn right (south). Proceed to stop sign at Cana Island Road at which point the road no longer goes straight. Turn right, following signs to the Spikehorn Camp Ground for approximately one mile where you will take a left turn following the Camp Ground signs. You will pass through the Camp Grounds. At this point the road narrows and becomes wooded as you approach the rocky causeway. Parking space is limited. Please be courteous to local land owners and respect their property lines and privacy. Hours: 10-5 daily. A nominal admission fee is charged.

Cana Island Lighthouse

69

A raging storm on November 18, 1958, sank the 638-foot Great Lakes freighter Carl D. Bradley in northern Lake Michigan, three and a half-hours after the ship had turned northeast from the landmark Cana Island Lighthouse. Winds up to seventy miles an hour and waves twenty-five to thirty feet high sent thirty-three sailors to a cold, watery death.

⚓

70

Old Baileys Harbor Lighthouse

Old Baileys Harbor Lighthouse birdcage lantern

Old Baileys Harbor Lighthouse

The Old Baileys Harbor Lighthouse has a direct connection to Justice Bailey, for whom the harbor is named. Captain Bailey, a schooner pilot, came upon this harbor during a storm in October of 1848. Originally named Gibraltar, Baileys Harbor is Door County's oldest village, more than 150 years old. The harbor here is natural and one of the finest on the Great Lakes. In its early days, Baileys Harbor was a significant Door County lumbering town, building stone supplier, and shipping port.

This forty-foot-high lighthouse was built in 1851-1852 on a tiny peninsula on North Point Island, sometimes called Lighthouse Island, at the eastern entrance to Baileys Harbor from Lake Michigan. History records that the water level was so low that construction supplies were hauled over the dry lakebed. The rocks used in the circular tower are large, flat, and light-colored, harvested from the immediate area. Old Baileys Harbor Lighthouse was built by Alanson Sweet, the owner of the shipping line with which Captain Bailey sailed. Mr. Sweet personally petitioned the federal government to erect this lighthouse. The light first saw service in the autumn of 1852.

The lantern room is an example of an old rare "bird cage" design, so called because it does resemble a bird cage from a distance. This unusual lantern room is one of only three surviving on the Great Lakes today. One remains on Lake Ontario and two on Lake Michigan, including this one. The bird cage lantern room was occasionally used in the 1850s prior to the fitting of most lights with Fresnel lenses. Polygonal lanterns became the norm a decade later. An Argand lamp with a reflector was the usual light source for the bird cage-style lantern room.

71

Current status: Not in operation. Erroneously called ruins, only the upper portion of the light has deteriorated and is in precarious shape. The house and tower are in excellent condition. The property is now privately owned and accessible only by boat. Please respect the privacy of the owners. They were gracious enough to allow us to photograph this Door County original up close.

How to get there: In Baileys Harbor go north on Highway 57 to Ridges Road (there will be a sign directing you to the Baileys Harbor Yacht Club). Turn right (east) onto Ridges Rd. Go approximately 1.5 miles, Ridges Rd. will curve to the left while the road to the Yacht club will continue straight. Stay on Ridges Rd. for approximately .5 mile to where it meets Harbor Lane. Stay on Ridges Road for another .5 mile until the road ends. This is a private, residential area where you can pull off the road to park. The lighthouse can be viewed on your right from an open area directly ahead of where the road ends. You can also view the lighthouse tower from Anclam Park in Baileys Harbor, or Baileys Harbor Ridges County Park and public beach on Ridge Road just off Hwy. 57 in Baileys Harbor (adjacent to the Ridges Sanctuary).

For years, this was the only lighthouse on the Door Peninsula, standing on a point at the far eastern end of the village of Baileys Harbor. Its poor location, however, doomed it to a short life. It did not provide a safe entrance around the many tricky shoals to Baileys Harbor. Used until 1870 when the Baileys Harbor Front and Rear Range Lights were lighted, the Old Baileys Harbor Lighthouse was rendered obsolete and remained abandoned for many years. During this time it changed hands several times.

Baileys Harbor Range Lights

This rather odd-looking set of buildings is a unique duo of Wisconsin lights. The Baileys Harbor Range Lights were built to allow mariners a safer harbor passage than the Old Baileys Harbor Lighthouse afforded. The lights guided vessels in a northwesterly direction through the treacherous shallows and reefs of the bay. Only a handful of lights of similar style exist on the Great Lakes. The lights are located in what is now the Ridges Sanctuary, a popular Door County natural area.

The Front or Lower Range Light, built in 1869, was first lit the following year. Closer to the water, the two-story, white and dark green structure rests just a few hundred feet from the shores of Baileys Harbor. At twenty-one feet tall it has the distinction of being the shortest lighthouse in Wisconsin. The first level is four-sided, while the second story is octagonal. The Front Range

Baileys Harbor Front Range Light

Light exhibited a steady red light, out its small rectangular window, which was modified several times over the years. The original boards of the Lower Light have also been replaced. The lantern was removed in 1969, after a hundred years of lighting the way.

The Rear or Upper Range Lighthouse was built the same year as the Front Range Light. A story-and-a-half white and red building, the thirty-five-foot-tall dwelling resembles an old country schoolhouse. This seven-room home housed the keeper and his family. The Rear Range Light is located 950 feet further inland from the Front Range Light, down a narrow corridor with a boardwalk. A beacon was situated in a small cupola atop the residence. A fifth-order Fresnel lens produced a steady white light that was fueled by lard or whale oil. When entering the harbor, seamen knew to keep the more elevated white light of the Rear Range Light directly over the red light of the lower Front Range Light. The Range Lights had a range of approximately twelve miles. Additionally, the Range Light grounds included a brick fuel-storage building and a two-seater outhouse (no waiting!). The buildings are listed on the National Register of Historic Places.

A handful of keepers made the Range Lights their home. The first was Fabien Truedell. Joseph Harris, Jr. was another of the early keepers of the Range Lights. The junior Mr. Harris and his wife became the parents of the first child born there. Mr. Joseph Harris, Sr. was a chief proponent of a ship canal that would eventually connect Sturgeon Bay with Lake Michigan. Unfortunately for

After the lights were automated, the Baileys Harbor Rear Range Lighthouse at one time served as a Lutheran Church minister's residence.

73

Baileys Harbor Rear Range Light

Baileys Harbor, the completion of the Sturgeon Bay Ship Canal in 1881-1882 had a grossly negative impact on the town's economy. Its days as a prominent shipping center in Door County were numbered.

Henry Gattie was another interesting keeper. His tenure at Baileys Harbor spanned almost three decades. In addition to his lighthouse duties he was responsible for all building maintenance, yard work, painting, and repairs. Since kerosene was strictly rationed, the light would be extinguished as soon as possible at dawn. Keeper Gattie managed both the Front and Rear Range Lights. When he was not at home, his wife Eva completed the lighting tasks. Picture in your mind the devoted keeper and family faithfully walking the lengthy boardwalk, day in and day out, hands gripping lantern fuel containers.

The 1920s and 1930s marked a significant turning point for the Range Lights. In the early 1920s an automated acetylene gas system was put in place, the buildings were locked up, and a keeper's presence was no longer required. The operation and upkeep of the Range Lights came under the jurisdiction of the keeper at Cana Island Light, four miles to the north. Electricity came to the Range Lights in 1930. Additionally in the 1930s the Door County Park Commission received permission from the Lighthouse Service to use most of the land surrounding the Range Lights. Controversy followed when the swales between the ridges near the beacons were scheduled to be filled with stone for future development. Because this area has unique botanical features, including many species of rare orchids, and uncommon geology, a group of far-sighted individuals formed the Ridges Sanctuary in the late 1930s to protect the area. The Ridges Sanctuary became Wisconsin's first National Natural Landmark in 1967. Over the years the Ridges has undertaken extensive renovations to keep the Baileys Harbor Range Lights in good repair.

As the 1960s drew to a close, the Range Lights became obsolete. Their function was transferred to a light and daymarker atop a metal tower nearer the lakeshore. Navigational buoys also were placed in Baileys Harbor. After a century of faithful service, the Baileys Harbor Range Lights' usefulness was over. For many local residents it was a sad passing.

Current status: Inactive. A modern metal tower exhibits a white light that flashes every 2.5 seconds. The historic range lights are part of the 800-acre Ridges Sanctuary, a privately held, non-profit nature preserve dedicated to preservation and education. The Ridges features ecologically significant swales and ridges, many species of orchids, and threatened and endangered plants. The Upper Range Light serves as a part-time residence and office for Ridges Sanctuary staff. Self-guided tours along the walking paths at the Ridges Sanctuary take you to the Range Lights. Listed on the National Register of Historic Places, the Range Lights can be viewed by the public year-round. During the annual Door County Lighthouse walk in mid-May, the buildings are open to the public and small beacons are again lit and shine out to the harbor. For further information, contact the Ridges Sanctuary at P.O. Box 152, Baileys Harbor, WI 54202 or call (920)-839-2802.

How to get there: In Baileys Harbor, turn east at the Sandpiper Restaurant on the corner of Hwy. 57 and Ridges Road. There is also a sign here directing you to the Baileys Harbor Yacht Club. Go approximately 0.3 of a mile. The Front Range Light will be on your immediate left with the Rear Range Light down a boardwalk path behind it.

Sturgeon Bay

Sturgeon Bay is a slender fish-shaped body of water lying near the midpoint of the Door peninsula. Reportedly named for its resemblance to the ancient sturgeon or possibly for the abundance of this fish in surrounding waters, Sturgeon Bay was Door County's first community, settled in 1835. Early economic activities included fur trading, lumbering, fishing, limestone quarrying, and ice harvesting in winter. Shipbuilding became the backbone of the local economy in the 1890s, and the city continues to be one of the largest shipbuilding centers on the Great Lakes today. Sturgeon Bay is the county's most populous city and the county seat.

The Sturgeon Bay Ship Canal

The building of the Sturgeon Bay Ship Canal, connecting Sturgeon Bay with Lake Michigan, had a profound influence on Door County maritime traffic as well as the status of several lighthouses on the peninsula. This project impacted existing lights and made additional beacons necessary. Negatively affected were Baileys Harbor shipping in general and the Baileys Harbor Range Lights in particular. New lighthouses included the Sturgeon Bay Canal North Pierhead Light, Canal Lighthouse, and the Sherwood Point Light.

The idea of excavating a ship canal was controversial in the early 1870s. Originally the government was not eager to become embroiled in the debate over the proposed channel. Finally, officials were persuaded that the canal would offer refuge to mariners. The government sanctioned studies and provided the capital for the canal and for harbor improvements. These enhancements were consolidated into the canal project. The Sturgeon Bay Ship Canal construction started in 1872 and was finished nearly a decade later, in 1881-1882. In excess of a million cubic yards of earth, rock, and lumber were removed. Total cost of the canal approached $300,000. Sea captains appreciated that the eleven-mile passage would avoid the risky Port des Morts strait and cut seventy miles from trips to ports in Milwaukee and Chicago.

courtesy Milwaukee Public Library

Dunlap Reef Lighthouse

Sturgeon Bay Ship Canal
North Pierhead Light

The Sturgeon Bay Ship Canal secured Sturgeon Bay's place as a deep-water port. With the completion of the canal in 1881, the United States Lighthouse Board sanctioned a lighthouse as well as a fog signal at this location. It marks the east entrance and mouth of Sturgeon Bay into Lake Michigan.

The original pier light atop a white tower was initially lit in 1882 and rested on the end of a wharf projecting out into Lake Michigan. This white open-skeleton tower was thirty-nine feet tall and possessed a sixth-order Fresnel lens that exhibited a steady red light. Access to the light was gained via a raised catwalk on the pier. Later two separate fog signal buildings were added near the shore, with blasts loud enough to be heard up to a dozen miles away.

In 1903 the Lighthouse Board ordered significant alterations at this station. The fog signal buildings and pierhead light were incorporated into the existing multi-storied lighthouse and fog signal building which stands forty-three feet tall. The new building was originally white in color, but later its hue was changed to red. Nicknamed "Big Red" (several Great Lakes lights share this name), the newer lantern most likely boasted the same sixth-order Fresnel lens taken from the original framework tower.

Sturgeon Bay was home to a virtually unknown Door County light, the Dunlap Reef Lighthouse. Only a select group of local residents know that two beacons, approximately 1,500 feet apart, formed a range light setup west of the old Sturgeon Bay bridge. Water depths in the area were dangerously shallow. Built in the 1870s and removed in the 1920s, a small beacon constituted the lower light while the upper light was a typical two-story framed house complete with light tower. When the crib structure supporting the main lighthouse eventually needed extensive rehabilitation, it was determined that the lights would be removed. The lighthouse, minus the light tower, was incorporated into a local Sturgeon Bay yard. Reportedly it is difficult to tell that the dwelling was ever a lighthouse. Buoys now mark the hazardous reef.

76

A lifesaving station was constructed along the canal west of the pier light before the turn of the century. It eventually became a significant U.S. Coast Guard Station that continues in operation today.

Current status: Active aid to navigation. The modern red light flashes every 2.5 seconds, visible for nine miles. Fog signal sounds a two-second blast every 30 seconds. The Coast Guard still accesses the light via the catwalk that runs the length of the pier and then spans over 20 feet of open water to where the lighthouse rests on the north pier. The light is not open to the public.

How to get there: From Hwy. 42/57 in Sturgeon Bay turn east just north of Bay View Bridge onto Utah St. Go approximately 0.4 mile, following the road as it goes right onto Cove Road. Now travel 0.3 mile to Canal Road. Turn left onto Canal Road and go approximately 2.5 miles to the Coast Guard Station. There are many overlooks of the canal along Canal Road. You will find a parking lot on your right.

The pierhead light can also be seen from Sturgeon Bay Canal Park, immediately south of the canal. Sand dunes still exist today along the Lake Michigan shoreline south of the Ship Canal.

Directions: From Hwy. 42/57, south of Sturgeon Bay, turn south onto County U (also known as Clay Banks Rd.). At a fork in the road proceed left, remaining on County U. Watch for Sand Lane, turn left onto Sand. Then take another left onto Lake Lane. Proceed east to Sturgeon Bay Canal Park. The park entrance, not easily seen, is just before a hard right turn onto Lake Michigan Drive.

77

Sturgeon Bay Ship Canal North Pierhead Light

Sturgeon Bay Ship Canal Lighthouse

After less than a decade of operation the light on the east end of the Sturgeon Bay Ship Canal was found to be inadequate. Seafarers demanded a stronger and more elevated beacon at the canal passage. Completed in 1899, a unique, non-supported tower eight feet in diameter was built of steel. Bracing wires were added later for support but vibration problems plagued this light. Because the lighthouse could not endure the shaking from the intense Lake Michigan winds, the Lighthouse Board authorized in 1903 the structural skeletal steel lattice work that today braces the bottom of the lighthouse tower. The inner steel tower supports the winding stairway of 115 interior steps. The tower, just under a hundred feet in height, contained a third-order Fresnel lens and flashed alternately white and red. The Canal Lighthouse was automated in 1972.

Giant thousand-foot ore carriers proceed through the ship canal regularly. In windy conditions, captains maneuver their vessels delicately, like trying to "thread a needle" in the narrow channel past the lighthouse.

⚓

78

Current status: Active aid to navigation. Today a third-order Fresnel lens is still in use. This fully operational light is part of the bustling U. S. Coast Guard Station. The grounds are beautifully maintained. The red rotating light flashes every ten seconds, visible for 17 miles. Scores of swallows make the light tower their home and there are numerous mud nests under the lantern room. Contact the US Coast Guard, 2501 Canal Rd, Sturgeon Bay, WI 54235.

How to get there: Located at the Lake Michigan end of the Sturgeon Bay Ship Canal. From Hwy. 42/57 in Sturgeon Bay turn east just north of Bay View Bridge onto Utah St. Go approximately 0.4 mile following the road as it goes right onto Cove Road. Now travel 0.3 mile to Canal Road. Turn left onto Canal Road and go approximately 2.5 miles to the Coast Guard Station. There are many overlooks of the canal along Canal Road. You will find a parking lot on your right. There is also a trail leading to the pierhead light directly ahead through the Coast Guard grounds. Please remain on the trail since this is a working Coast Guard Station. You will be able to see both lights with ease from this location.

The Light station can also be seen from Sturgeon Bay Canal Park, immediately south of the canal. Directions: From Hwy. 42/57, south of Sturgeon Bay, turn south onto County U (also known a Clay Banks Rd.). At a fork in the road proceed left, remaining on County U. Watch for Sand Lane, turn left onto Sand. Then take another left onto Lake Lane. Proceed east to Sturgeon Bay Canal Park. The park entrance, not easily seen, is just before a hard right turn onto Lake Michigan Drive.

following page: Sturgeon Bay Ship Canal Lighthouse

80

Fresnel Lens, Cana Island Lighthouse

Other Lake Michigan Lights

The remainder of Wisconsin's "east coast" is dotted with many lighthouses of historic and contemporary significance. It seems that nearly every major Wisconsin coastline city, especially those with rivers that connected to the big lake, has a lighthouse. Every twenty to twenty-five miles or so you can be sure to find these Lake Michigan lights.

As shipping increased in the 1840s, harbors were developed in most Wisconsin ports. The area from Sturgeon Bay to Manitowoc became a hub for fishing, shipping, and the building of large boats. Wind and steam powered the earliest vessels. Two Rivers and Kewaunee were active in the fishing trade. Within twenty years many of these port towns made their harbors more useful by dredging and extending piers further into the lake, so that larger ships could dock. The cities of Manitowoc and Kewaunee became car ferry ports in the 1890s, transporting railroad cars and their goods to Michigan. Wooden freighters were constructed in Manitowoc, making this city a major shipbuilding center.

Harbor at sunset

Algoma North Pierhead Light

The settlement in this area was first named Ahnapee, taking its name from the river that joins Lake Michigan here. Algoma comes from a Native American name meaning "park of flowers."

The first lighthouse was built here at the harbor entrance in 1893 for the "protection and guidance of shipping" and was named the Ahnapee Light Station. Situated at the mouth of the Ahnapee River, the lighthouse was placed into service on March 1, 1893. Vitally important to the commerce of Algoma, the original light was a square, pyramid-shaped white wooden tower twenty-two feet in height. An open framework made up the lower portion of the light, while the upper portion had an enclosed watch room and a black hexagonal iron lantern. Oil was burned to illuminate this original harbor light with red lens. It was visible for only two or three miles in clear weather. Ole Hansen became the first lightkeeper in 1893. His residence sat atop a bluff on the north side of the harbor.

The light was reconstructed in 1908, and in 1932 the tower was positioned on a new base, increasing the height of the structure to forty-two feet. Two separate observation railings circle the light tower, one midway up, the other surrounding the lantern area. The current round red metal lighthouse is the symbol of Algoma.

Louis Braemer devoted thirty-one of his thirty-six years in the Lighthouse Service at Algoma, beginning in 1910 and ending twenty-nine years later. He routinely worked twelve-hour days. Stories of his love for Algoma and his chores of cleaning the kerosene film off the lighthouse windows, painting the lighthouse, and polishing the brass equipment of the lighthouse can be found in archival materials on the light. His daughter recalled the lighthouse always smelled of polish.

A raised catwalk ran the length of the pier from the shore to the light so the keeper could safely access the oil lamp in any kind of weather. The catwalk was especially treacherous in storms and icy conditions. Records exist of thick ice covering the catwalk many times during the winter months. A fifth-order Fresnel lens and larger oil lamp were installed in 1895 and overhauled in 1908. The light station was fitted with a gasoline-powered fog signal on April 5, 1910. It had been reported that until the foghorn was installed mariners became quite frustrated trying to find the Algoma harbor on extremely foggy days.

The light station was updated in 1932 when the U.S. government began a harbor improvement project, which consisted of a new 1,100-foot-long concrete North pier, a new fog signal, and new steel lighthouse tower. This light is one of only a select Wisconsin duo, the other being the Sturgeon Bay Ship Canal North Pierhead Light, to still utilize a catwalk. Approximately fifty men, at least half of them from Algoma, worked on the construction project to update the light. One account claims that General Douglas MacArthur supervised the Algoma project, another that, as an engineer, he helped to design the pier. The light was automated in 1973.

There do not appear to be any catastrophes directly associated with the Algoma Light, but a tragic tale does involve one of its lightkeepers. Gustavus (Gus) Umberham was keeper here from 1901 to 1913. He earned fifty dollars a month, which in those days provided a comfortable living. Umberham drowned on February 3, 1913, while returning from Kewaunee in inclement weather via boat with several friends on a cold, dark evening. Using the Kewaunee and Algoma Lights as guides, the group headed north. The wind and waves were jostling their boat. Umberham apparently lost his balance and fell headfirst into the lake. Only two shouts from Umberham were heard before Lake Michigan's icy waters snuffed out his life. The death of Umberham was a shock to the town of Algoma, engulfing it in sadness for some time.

Current status: Active aid to navigation. A red isophase light from a fifth-order Fresnel lens cycles three seconds on, three seconds off, with a 48-foot focal plane, visible for 16 miles. Fog signal sounds a one-second blast every 10 seconds.

How to get there: The light is located at the end of North Pier-Algoma Harbor at the mouth of the Ahnapee River. Enjoy a scenic half-mile stroll along the handicapped-accessible Crescent Beach Boardwalk. For further information contact the Algoma Area Chamber of Commerce Visitors Center, which overlooks Lake Michigan, 1226 Lake St. (Highway 42) Algoma, WI. 54201. Phone (800) 498-4888 or (920) 487-2041. On the web, www.algoma.org. Or visit the Algoma Public Library.

Kewaunee

Nestled south of Door County, the name Kewaunee traces its origins to the Potawatomi. They would call out from their canoes a similar-sounding phrase that meant "we are lost" when they could not find their location in a Lake Michigan fog. The Kewaunee River also played an important role in the history of this region. Kewaunee's natural harbor attracted Native Americans as well as European traders and trappers. The current channel was dredged in approximately 1892. Logging was an important early industry in Kewaunee.

Originally a set of two range lights, built in 1891, guided mariners into port. These lights no longer exist. According to Kewaunee Historical Society Curator Tom Schuller, prior to having a fog signal on the old lighthouse the lightkeeper would walk to the end of the pier and bang a board on the pier or house to warn sailors in the fog. A more effective fog signal building was constructed in 1909. A seventy-foot steel range light tower followed in 1912. A Coast Guard Station existed near the harbor entrance at Kewaunee, just upstream of the lighthouse.

Kewaunee Pierhead Lighthouse

The present pierhead light is located on the end of the reinforced concrete south pier. Opposite the channel is another navigational marker. The old front range light was eliminated in 1931 when a new four-sided tower was built on the crown of the 1909 fog signal complex. The current optic, a fifth-order Fresnel lens, may have come from the original 1891 light.

At one time an elevated catwalk ran the length of the cement pier and provided safer access to the light in inclement weather. The Kewaunee Pierhead Light was used to direct ferry service between Ludington, Michigan, and Kewaunee. The Wisconsin port was later moved south to Manitowoc for economic reasons. The lighthouse was automated in 1981. A radio antenna still towers above the lantern room today.

The car ferry Ann Arbor *crashed head-on into the south pier in 1930. The pier was demolished and the lighthouse damaged. The Army Corps of Engineers repaired the pierhead after the collision.*

84

Current status: Active aid to navigation. Fully operational year-round. A fifth-order Fresnel lens exhibits a brilliant white, fixed light, 43-foot focal plane, visible for 15 miles. Fog signal sounds a three-second blast every 30 seconds.

How to get there: Follow highway 42, the main road that goes through downtown Kewaunee. Approximately 4 blocks south of the Kewaunee River, turn east onto Ellis St. Proceed east till the road ends, about 3 blocks. You can walk out to the lighthouse on the end of the south breakwater.

Kewaunee Pierhead Lighthouse

85

Rawley Point Lighthouse

Rawley Point is a seemingly gentle protrusion of sand into Lake Michigan, about five miles north of the city of Two Rivers. Masking treacherous shoals that have been the cause of more than two dozen shipwrecks, the lighthouse here stands as a warning signal to potential future victims who venture too close to shore. This light has been given multiple names, including Twin River Point Light, Twin Rivers Light, Point Beach Light, and Two Rivers Lighthouse.

Located in Manitowoc County, this tip of land was named after Peter Rowley, who settled in this region in 1835. He operated a trading post and did a profitable business with the local Ottawa and Potawatomi. During the early 1840s U.S. government surveyors asked Mr. Rowley the name of this point. He did not tell them he had named the area Mink River. The surveyors knew Mr. Rowley was one of the first prominent European settlers in this locale so they named it Rowley Point. At some point the spelling was changed to Rawley on navigational maps and charts.

It is not clear exactly when a lighthouse was first constructed here. Records indicate that the first lighthouse in this general area was built in 1854 at Twin River Point. The first lighthouse at this particular location was built about twenty years later. The original brick light tower stood eighty-five feet tall and was attached to the keeper's dwelling by a hallway. On the north end of the present-day keeper's dwelling, the remains of the original circular tower can still be seen. In 1895 the top portion of that tower was demolished and the shorter tower then became part of the keeper's quarters. One result is a curious round living room that may be seen today. A fire damaged the keeper's quarters on a frigid January 1, 1962. Also located on the grounds, closer to the lake, was a steam-whistle foghorn, powered by a boiler, which produced a deafening, shrill tone followed by the familiar, low, and mournful "gar-um-umph" noise.

In 1941 an assistant keeper at Rawley Point Lighthouse died of a heart attack immediately after having climbed and descended the tower.

The current eight-sided pyramidal erector style lighthouse, the only one of this type on the Great Lakes, stands 111 feet, the second tallest lighthouse in Wisconsin. It is an alteration and expansion of a lighthouse taken from the Chicago River in 1893 after the World's Fair. The light tower has a central iron-stair cylinder, containing 132 stairs, with support supplied by a maze of exterior steel frames. There is a double-decker set of watchrooms with ornate fencing, placed one atop the other, below the lantern room. These dual watchrooms are another unique feature among Wisconsin lights. The light tower was constructed next to the two-and-a-half-story keeper's quarters. From the late 1800s until 1920, vapor lamps were used to light the way for sailors. The original seven-foot tall, third-order Fresnel lens revolved on a metal roller and was wound every six hours by heavy weights. This station had a radio beacon and was an important monitoring station that kept track of many other radio beacons on Lake Michigan and Green Bay. Modern ships could plot their position by radio signals. At the time, this was an important method of navigation.

The light was electrified in 1920. The original lens was in use until 1952, when a piece of the lens broke and was replaced with the current twin-bull's-eye rotating beacon that can be seen for twenty-eight miles, with 300,000 candlepower. Look out over Lake Michigan and imagine the shipwrecks off this unassuming point. The worst in the immediate area occurred in October, 1887. The *Vernon*, a large passenger steamer, sank in bad weather with the loss of three dozen lives.

preceding page: Rawley Point Lighthouse

Current status: Active aid to navigation. White light flashes every 15 seconds with a rotating bullseye beacon, 113-foot focal plane, visible for 28 miles. No fog signal. Today the well-kept quarters are off limits and currently utilized by the Coast Guard for housing and as a military recreation cottage. The boarded-up white outbuilding east of the lighthouse is all that remains of the old fog signal building. The lighthouse is not open to the public but the grounds are easily accessed from the nearly 3,000-acre Point Beach State Park. An admission fee to the park is charged. Walk the sand beach and the gentle rolling dunes to view the light.

How to get there: At Hwy. 42 and 22nd St. (County Rd. O) drive east on 22nd St. approximately four blocks. Turn left (north) on O and follow signs to Point Beach State Park, approximately 4.5 miles. A right turn will take you into the park and another .25 mile to the park information booth. All visitors must pay the daily park admission fee or have a current annual park sticker. The lighthouse is immediately east of the park entrance office and parking lot. A map of the park is available at the park entrance.

Two Rivers

Like many fledgling Wisconsin lakeshore communities, Two Rivers merchants and manufacturers long ago pushed for commercial development of the city's harbor, one of the most accessible in the region. Harbor development included dredging and the building of two parallel piers and a lighthouse. A volunteer lifesaving station also was established in the 1870s. Today, Two Rivers is a center for both sport and commercial fishing. Whitefish, trout, smelt, and alewives have long been plentiful here.

Two Rivers North Pierhead Light

This proud beacon, now in the popular Rogers Street Fishing Village, has been adopted as the official symbol of Two Rivers. The light was erected in Manitowoc County by a local builder. The townspeople thought the lighthouse construction was done well, but the contractor "did the work too cheap," according to contemporary records. The red wooden structure stood approximately thirty-six feet tall at the end of the North Pier of the Two Rivers Harbor and was first lit in the autumn of 1886. A sixth-order Fresnel lens, standing about a foot tall, was enclosed in a solid brass housing. The lens had an area of coverage of 240 degrees and was lit with an oil-fired lamp. Its signature was a fixed red light. The lighthouse featured a diaphone foghorn with a distinctly deep, two-tone pitch. An elevated catwalk led to a doorway on the side of the framed lighthouse, allowing the keeper a safer journey to and from the light during bad weather. The light was tended by the Rawley Point lightkeeper who lived five miles to the north. Completely rebuilt in 1928 after it had been deteriorated by the elements, the lamp gave off light equivalent to more than a hundred candlepower.

following page: Two Rivers North Pierhead Light

This light was retired in 1969 and replaced by a three-story steel structure and foghorn, the new light displaying the familiar, fixed red character. The U.S. Coast Guard donated the lantern room and upper section of the old light to the Two Rivers Historical Society and the people of the community. Unfortunately, the Fresnel lens was broken when the lighthouse was moved. The old light is mounted atop a wooden base. You may climb a stairway to an observation platform to get a better view of the East Twin River portion of the Two Rivers harbor. The area where the pier light rests, called Lighthouse Park, is adjacent to Rogers St..

The Rogers Street Fishing Village, home of the lighthouse today, marks the location of the Two Rivers fleet, which fished these waters as far back as the 1830s. The lighthouse, given a second life, is now the focal point of the Historic Rogers Street Fishing Village Museum, which seeks to preserve and depict the lifestyle of lake fishermen. Listed on the National Register of Historic Places, the museum offers self-guided tours of the lighthouse and also features a replica of an engine room, a Lake Michigan fishing tug, the *Buddy O*, and an assortment of old photographs and fishing artifacts. The museum is open 10 a.m. to 4 p.m. daily, May through October, and by appointment from November through April. Contact the Museum, 2102 Jackson St., P.O. Box 33, Two Rivers, WI. 54241. Tel. (920) 793-5905. The museum is operated with donations only.

On November 13, 1912, the vessel Rouse Simmons, also known as the "Christmas tree ship," bringing a load of holiday trees from Michigan to Chicago, sank off Two Rivers in a fierce storm. A note retrieved from a bottle found near Sheboygan contained the last written words of the doomed captain, Herman Schuenemann. "Everybody good-by. I guess we are (sic) thru. Leaking bad. Endwald and Steve fell overboard. God help us." The anchor of the Rouse Simmons today adorns the entrance to the Milwaukee Yacht Club.

Current status: Inactive. Part of local fishing museum.

How to get there: From the south, take Hwy. 42 through downtown Two Rivers. Highway 42 becomes Washington St. Cross over the West Twin River. Proceed approximately 0.7 mile where Highway 42 takes a right (east) turn at 22nd St. Go about 0.3 mile, cross the bridge over the East Twin River, and turn right (south) immediately at Jackson St., the first street after you cross the bridge. The lighthouse and Fishing Village Museum will be on your immediate right.

From the north, take Hwy 42 (Lincoln Ave.) south to 22nd St. Within two blocks is Jackson St. Turn left (south) onto Jackson. The lighthouse and Fishing Village Museum will be on your immediate right.

Manitowoc

Manitowoc is derived from a Native American term meaning "home of the great spirit." The earliest mention of Manitowoc was recorded by Col. Abraham Edwards in 1818 while canoeing with others along the Lake Michigan shore. He and his party observed Native Americans spearfishing. In 1835 the Menominee sold this territory to the U.S. government. Within two years settlers from Europe arrived. New communities were born and sawmills were built. With lumber to be shipped, a lighthouse was soon to come.

Manitowoc, long known as a shipbuilding center, has always had a rich maritime history. In the 1800s it built schooners, and in later years military landing craft, submarines, and yachts. Today Manitowoc refers to itself as "Wisconsin's maritime capitol."

One of the first Lake Michigan lights, the original Manitowoc lighthouse was built in 1840 on high ground at the Manitowoc River estuary. A decade later a wooden, pyramid-shaped lighthouse was constructed on the end of a long pier. Access was gained via an elevated catwalk. In 1854 the light was moved to the mouth of the river. It was destroyed by a storm in 1937.

Manitowoc North Breakwater Lighthouse

The first light to mark the end of the Manitowoc breakwater was constructed in 1895. The current steel breakwater light, located on the end of the north breakwater, was built in 1918 and stands fifty feet tall on a concrete jetty. At that time the lighthouse also had a catwalk leading to shore. The tri-layered construction of the lighthouse has been compared to a tiered cake. The original lens was a fourth-order Fresnel, but currently a fifth-order Fresnel lens rises above Lake Michigan. A modern plastic lens sits outside the lantern room serving as a back-up to the dependable Fresnel. The building has a fog signal, which is enclosed in the first level of the lighthouse, and the second floor is an observation area. A two-story radio antenna still protrudes skyward from the lantern room area. The Breakwater Lighthouse was automated in the early 1970s.

The Manitowoc Breakwater Light historically has served to guide many vessels in and out of the harbor. Currently it also guides the *S.S. Badger*, the only remaining car ferry on Lake Michigan. The boat departs daily on the four-hour journey to Ludington, Michigan, mid-May through mid-October.

For additional information telephone 1-800-841-4243 or 1-888-947-3377 or on the Internet at www.ssbadger.com.

Manitowoc is home to the Wisconsin Maritime Museum, the largest of its kind in the Midwest. Nautical history dating back more than a century comes alive here with many exhibits. Visitors may also tour a genuine WWII submarine, the *USS Cobia*. A fifth-order Fresnel lens from Manistique, Michigan, may be seen directly above your head as you enter the main door of the museum. This multi-million dollar facility is a must-see for the Great Lakes maritime buff. The Wisconsin Maritime Museum is located at 75 Maritime Dr. Phone (920) 684-0218.

92

Manitowoc North Breakwater Lighthouse

Current status: Active aid to navigation. A white isophase light from a fourth-order Fresnel lens cycles three seconds on and three seconds off; 52 foot focal plane, visible for 17 miles. The fog signal sounds two separate blasts in a 30-second period.

How to get there: West of Manitowoc, take Hwy. I-43 to Hwy. 151 (exit # 149). Hwy. 151 becomes Calumet Ave. At S. 26th St. turn left (north) and go about one block to Custer St. Turn right (east) onto Custer, which becomes Washington St. Proceed east on Washington to 10th St. Turn left (north) on 10th. You will cross the Manitowoc River. Immediately across the river is Maritime Drive. Turn right (east) on Maritime. This road winds past the Wisconsin Maritime Museum. On your right watch for the Manitowoc Marina signs. Plenty of parking is available. The lighthouse is not open, but you can walk right up to it. It is approximately a 15-minute trek to the lighthouse from the parking lot.

To view the lighthouse from the south across the bay, simply follow the "Car Ferry" signs in Manitowoc. This will lead you to a gravel parking lot by the car ferry dock. A cement walkway leads to a pierhead light directly across from the lighthouse. This walk is shorter than the one via the North breakwater pier.

Sheboygan

Sheboygan is located at the exact north-south center of the western shore of Lake Michigan. The Native American term *Sheub-wau-wau-gun*, meaning "where the river disappears under the ground," is probably the origin of the name Sheboygan. Early accounts of the city specifically mention the magnificent harbor. The mouth of the Sheboygan River was recognized early on as a vital natural harbor and quickly became a lifeblood resource to the community. A narrow sand bar, created by Lake Michigan waves, rested across the river's mouth where it joined the big lake. Native American tribes thrived along the riverbanks.

Sheboygan's business and manufacturing interests have relied on its Lake Michigan connection since the 1830s. The Sheboygan harbor was first dredged for commercial access in the 1850s. Nearly all of the city's goods and materials arrived by way of Lake Michigan. Some of the most important included coal, lumber and wood products, salt, fish, fruits, vegetables, and other agricultural products. Sheboygan was a shipbuilding city early in its history, and also was an automobile manufacturing center for a time. Today, Sheboygan continues its connection to the lake with a great sport fishing industry as well as other water-related recreation and commerce.

Sheboygan Breakwater Lighthouse

In 1839, the first lighthouse to serve the Sheboygan harbor was built on what was known as North Sheboygan Point. The keeper was a Mr. Wolverton. Alexander Hamilton Edwards also

The schooner Lottie Cooper *battled gale-force winds before capsizing and sinking just off the Sheboygan harbor in April, 1894. Over 130 feet in length with a five-story main mast, she was representative of the hundreds of commercial boats of that era. The reconstructed wooden wreck can be viewed in nearby Deland Park.*

Sheboygan Breakwater Lighthouse

94

served briefly in the late 1840s. This light with its fixed beacon stood for two decades before being replaced in 1860 by a newer version. Some years later the light had a woman keeper, a Mrs. E. Pape, whose keeper husband Louis Pape had been hurt in a Fourth of July cannon bursting accident. At the beginning of December 1873 a lighthouse on the north pier of the harbor was built. A fire engulfed that light on March 17, 1880, and three months later a new building replaced the burned structure.

Harbor improvements and an extension of the harbor pier were closely followed by the breakwater light. Originally this light was a cone-shaped metal tower, with a diameter of twelve and a half feet at its base. It was equipped with a cast iron lantern and was slightly more than fifty feet tall. The light was rebuilt and moved several times.

The present light was built in 1915. A skeletal steel pierhead tower was constructed off site that year and placed here. This was the typical pierhead style, topped with a circular parapet and lantern room. It is not known when or why the lantern room was removed.

Current status: Active aid to navigation. White light flashes every four seconds; 55-foot focal plane, visible for nine miles. Fog signal sounds a three-second blast in a 30 second period. The current light tower stands 50 feet tall and has a plastic lens but no lantern room. Also atop the tower are weather devices and a radio antenna. The former lantern area of the lighthouse serves as a National Data Buoy Center station, which measures air temperature, wind speed and direction, and atmospheric pressure.

How to get there: From I-43 west of Sheboygan take Hwy. 23 east (exit # 126). This is Kohler Memorial Drive. Kohler Memorial becomes Erie Ave. Continue on Erie approx. 1.25 miles to 4th St. where Erie ends. Turn right (south) onto 4th St. for two blocks. Turn left (east) on Niagara Ave. Go one block to Broughton Dr. Turn right (south) onto Broughton and go one and a half blocks to Wisconsin Ave. Turn left on Wisconsin. Watch for signs for Deland Park and the Harbor Centre Marina. Located at the harbor's north stone and concrete breakwall in Deland Park. Sheboygan's renovated lakefront and its excellent Harbor Centre Marina are wonderful places to take a leisurely stroll. The approximate .3 mile (10 minute) walk from the shore to the lighthouse is a favorite summer pastime for locals and visitors.

Port Washington

Originally known as Wisconsin City, Port Washington was founded in 1835 at the entrance to the Sauk River. Its early history is closely linked to Lake Michigan and the steamers that stopped here. By 1845 its first pier jutted several hundred feet out into the lake. The city's port has been dredged several times, the first in 1870. Port Washington had the first artificial harbor on the Great Lakes. Commercial fishing had long been an important part of this friendly city's local economy.

An 1849 map indicates the site of the original light to guide mariners into Port Washington. It was a circular Cream City brick light tower built on the North Bluff (St. Mary's Hill) along with a keeper's house. The land rose more than eighty feet above lake level, north of the harbor of Port Washington. In 1889 the first pierhead lighthouse was built.

Old Port Washington Light Station

This light station, approximately fifty feet tall, was built slightly west of Port Washington's first light tower. The date of construction, 1860, is still clearly marked on the front of the building today. The cream city brick house, built on a stone foundation, originally featured an oil-fueled beacon. A fixed white light from a fourth-order Fresnel lens was visible for nearly twenty miles. A brick oil house once existed on the property.

One of the more colorful characters in the light's early history was keeper Fontleroy Hoyt. A man of considerable height, he was accustomed to wearing a long linen duster complete with tails that would fly in the wind. Children called him "Fantail," a nickname that stuck.

Keeper Captain Charles H. Lewis, Sr., and his family performed the majority of years of service at the Old Port Washington

The lighthouse and accompanying harbor fog signal at Port Washington proved inadequate when two steamers, the Marquette *and* Senator *collided on October 31, 1929, in heavy fog. Ten lives and the* Senator *were lost.*

Lighthouse. Their tenure began in 1874 and lasted for more than six decades. Captain Lewis was a whaling skipper and Great Lakes sailor. His wife also served as lightkeeper for a year after his death in 1880. In 1881 their son, Charles, Jr., succeeded his parents as keeper, holding that position for forty-four years! The young Mr. Lewis was credited with saving many lives on Lake Michigan during his days here. He was also well known for being quite the storyteller and yarn spinner.

The keepers tending this station had double duty. In addition to keeping the light atop the hill, they journeyed to the wooden pyramidal pier light first lit in 1889 in the Port Washington harbor. The keepers were able to gain access to the harbor tower via a raised wooden catwalk. The old pier light was automated in 1924 and decommissioned in the 1930s.

After the Port Washington Breakwater Light was lit in 1935, the Old Port Washington Lighthouse became obsolete. The tower, lantern room, and widow's walk were removed. The light was discontinued on October 31,

courtesy Port Washington Historical Society

Old Port Washington Light Station

1903. The breathtaking view from the top of the lantern room would be no more. The building was redesigned into an upper and lower flat. Keepers of the new Breakwater Light continued to reside in the remodeled old light station. The buildings then housed Coast Guard personnel as tenders of the pierhead light. When the 1935 Breakwater Lighthouse and foghorn became fully automated in the mid-1970s, the light station continued to serve as housing for Coast Guard personnel from Milwaukee. In 1992 it was leased to the Port Washington Historical Society, and in 1998 ownership of the buildings and grounds were transferred to the city of Port Washington with oversight by the National Park Service. All told, the building has served in various capacities for nearly 140 years.

Old Port Washington Light Station today

Current status: Inactive. The building stands as a symbol of Port Washington's long maritime tradition. The two-story brick lighthouse is currently being restored by the Port Washington Historical Society and houses their local history museum featuring memorabilia from Port Washington's history of more than 160 years. It is listed on the State Register of Historic Buildings. After renovation is complete, a lantern room will once again sit proudly atop the house, affording a splendid view over Lake Michigan. The building is open for free tours on Sundays from 1 to 4 p.m. June through September, or by appointment at any time. Contact the Port Washington Historical Society, 311 Johnson St., Port Washington WI 53074. Phone: (262) 284-7240 or (262) 284-3755.

How to get there: From I-43 west of Port Washington take Hwy. 33 east (exit #96). Hwy. 33 becomes Grand Ave. Proceed for approximately 2.9 miles to Franklin St. in downtown Port Washington. Turn left (north) on Franklin St. Proceed 0.4 mile to Woodruff St. (At this point Franklin St. will now be called Wisconsin St. and Hwy 32 North). Turn right on Woodruff and go about 1/2 a block to N. Catalpa St, turn right. Catalpa St. curves past St. Mary's Church for about 1 block to Van Buren St. Turn right, proceed for another half block to Johnson St. Turn right on Johnson St. The road curves to the left. Proceed about two blocks on Johnson St. The old lighthouse is on the left side of the street, at 311 Johnson St.

Port Washington Breakwater Light

Port Washington had a dubious reputation of having one of the worst harbors on the Great Lakes. Millions of dollars in damages to vessels and the lakefront from storms was a recurring problem. Despite previous excavations, additional harbor enhancements in the 1930s including a breakwater and a new pierhead lighthouse were necessary. When the Port Washington Marina was completed in 1982, boaters finally had a safe harbor.

Located on the end of the north breakwater, this beacon is the symbol of Port Washington. In 1933 a new breakwater of steel, stone, and cement was constructed at a cost of $625,000. Arthur Almquist, with nearly two decades of lighthouse tending experience, became the first keeper of the new lighthouse. Built in 1935, it replaced the 1889 pier and light. The new structure was bargain-priced at $35,000. One of the newer lights in Wisconsin and on Lake Michigan, it possesses a unique art deco style. This unusual Badgerland light has a twin in an Indiana harbor. The two-story concrete foundation has reinforced arched openings on all four sides to allow high seas to pass beneath it without doing damage. The white steel lighthouse rises an additional forty feet and is wide at the connection to the four-legged base, then tapering to the top. Portholes are scattered throughout the tower. The light flashed a red signal every 7.5 seconds from a fourth-order Fresnel lens housed in a black lantern room, since removed. The accompanying deep-booming foghorn could be heard for eighteen miles.

The keeper who lived at the Old Port Washington Light Station atop St. Mary's hill overlooking the city tended this lighthouse. The keeper would trudge up and down the bluff to care for the foghorn, since the light was automatic. It's a safe bet the keeper got plenty of exercise. An attendant was no longer needed, however, when both the light and foghorn were totally automated in the mid-1970s.

Current status: Active aid to navigation. Today, a modern red plastic beacon tops the lighthouse. The red light flashes every six seconds. With a 78-foot focal plane, the light is visible for eight miles. The structure is also equipped with a fog signal, which is not as loud as the original drone. The fog signal sounds two blasts every thirty seconds.

How to get there: From I-43 west of Port Washington take Hwy. 33 east (exit #96). Hwy. 33 becomes Grand Ave. Proceed for approximately 2.9 miles to Franklin St. in downtown Port Washington. Go left (north) onto Franklin St. for approximately three blocks to Pier St. Turn right (east) onto Pier St. Go three blocks to the marina parking lot which will be directly in front of you. This parking lot is metered. Access to the walkway to the lighthouse is located at the foot of Jackson St. (one block north of Pier St.). The first part of the slightly less than half-mile walk to the light takes you on a narrow walkway with metal decking. A little further out you encounter uneven concrete and large boulders, then a smooth, three-foot-wide concrete walkway to the lighthouse.

Kevich Light

The youngest Wisconsin light, this private dwelling and attached lighthouse in Grafton were built in 1981. Kevich Light is perched high atop a bluff where a once bustling town, Port Ulao (pronounced: you-lee-o), existed. Today only faded memories remain of what has been called one of Wisconsin's ghost towns.

Towering atop the clay bluffs of Lake Michigan, Port Ulao was a significant anchorage and thriving village in the 1850s. Nestled between Port Washington and Milwaukee, Port Ulao was rich in forested land, the plateau above the lake being described as "one immense woodyard." An enterprising man, James T. Gifford, realizing the potential of the area and resource, cleared the land for farming and sold the lumber to lake steamers.

A request was made in the 1850s to the federal government to erect a lighthouse at Port Ulao. A small parcel of land was actually deeded in anticipation of a light, but there is no record of a lighthouse ever being built here in the nineteenth century. The port's chief importance was as a source of fuel for ships. A wooden pier stretched a thousand feet into the lake as a moorage for steamers loading fuel. The enterprising Mr. Gifford had a wooden trough constructed that funneled wood from the top of the bluff to the beach. Can you just imagine the sound of the cut wood roaring lakeward down the chute?

Kevich Light lamps

Port Ulao's importance lasted only as long as its timber resource. After much of the nearby lumber was felled, the port, lacking a lighthouse or harbor improvements, quickly withered.

Brana A. Kevich, an ordained Serbian Orthodox priest of Yugoslavian descent, built the forty-five-foot lighthouse you see today. Father Kevich fled his native Yugoslavia in the early 1950s, escaping into Austria after being shot at by Yugoslavian border guards. He built the light because "I wanted to help mankind and give people a light who needed it because God showed me His light in a Yugoslavian forest many years ago."

An accomplished student of architecture, Mr. Kevich specialized in hand-carved religious artwork. The doorway to the light tower features his woodcarvings. When Kevich was in residence, the house also included many of his crafts, including hand-chiseled doors, cabinets, tables, and chairs.

Kevich Light was upgraded with a larger lighting system in the early 1990s. A Fresnel lens was intended to be used, but one could not be found. Today the light source consists of two bulbs, one of four hundred watts, the other a thousand watts. Aluminum is used for much of the light mechanism. A shield revolves around the light every eight seconds, which causes the light to be illuminated for four seconds, followed by four seconds of darkness. This type of light timing is called an isophase characteristic.

following page: Kevich Light

Current status: Operational. A white isophase light cycles four seconds on and four seconds off. No fog horn. Privately owned and operated. Only a select number of private aids to navigation exist in the United States. Kevich Light is visible on Lake Michigan for nearly 20 miles. It stands 163 feet above lake level. Kevich Light was certified as a U.S. Coast Guard Class II Private Aid to Navigation in 1990. Officially the U.S. Coast Guard Light List designates Kevich Light as number 20765.
How to get there: At the owner's request, we are omitting directions to this light. Please respect their privacy. Visit the lighthouse via their web site at www.execpc.com/~portulao/

Milwaukee

The city's name is derived from the Potawatomi term *Mahn-ah-wauk* which means "gathering place by water." Milwaukee County was incorporated in 1835, the same year that the first steamship reached what would later become Milwaukee harbor. The harbor was officially established in the spring of 1843. Three years later Milwaukee became a city. Five more years would pass before Wisconsin became a state. Within two decades, Milwaukee was a major manufacturing center as well as a primary market for the shipment of wheat.

The first lighthouse to guard the Milwaukee Bay was built in 1837 on a fifty-six-foot-high bluff at the head of Wisconsin St. (now Wisconsin Ave.) and Lake St. (now Lake Drive). The bluff's slope was diminished long ago when portions of the ravines were filled in. The light was intended to mark the Milwaukee River's entrance but was built further north by nearly a mile and offered little help to navigation. It did, however, serve as a favorite gambling establishment and watering hole for the keeper, Eli Bates. He is reported to have exceeded his $300 annual lightkeeper's salary in liquor and tobacco sales and gambling receipts. The original Milwaukee light was demolished in 1855.

Unknown even to most native Milwaukeeans, prior to the building of the Milwaukee Breakwater Lighthouse the city had its own lightship, vessel number 95. For nearly two decades it served to guide countless mariners to the port of Milwaukee. Anchored nearly three miles out from the harbor in the open lake, lonely crews gladly welcomed visitors who would come out to visit the strange sheet-iron vessel. A tubular mast amidships supported the large beacon perched atop. The lightship was removed from service after the Milwaukee Breakwater Lighthouse and its radio beacon came on line in 1926.

North Point Lighthouse

This Milwaukee County light, whose name comes from the northern limit of Milwaukee Bay, is located in scenic Lake Park on Milwaukee's East Side. The lighthouse is one of only a handful of lights located within a major city. Consisting of 140 acres, Lake Park, a registered national landmark, was designed more than a century ago by Frederick Law Olmstead, the renowned master landscape planner for Central Park in New York City. By the turn of the twentieth century Lake Park was THE place to be. One of the top cultural and social gathering places in Milwaukee, horse-drawn carriage rides, bicycling, and free band concerts were commonplace. Hundreds of people enjoyed the park's beauty. Electric trolley cars ferried people to and from the park. Today people continue to enjoy the park's paths, wooded areas, ravines, and golf course.

The timing of the choice of this site for a new lighthouse coincided with plans that were being drawn up to make an artificial "straight cut" connection of the Milwaukee River and Lake Michigan. The original North Point Light, first lit November 22, 1855, was a twenty-eight-foot yellow brick structure that stood closer to the bluff than does the lighthouse we view at this site today. At that time it was the highest light on the Great Lakes, more than a hundred feet above lake level, and today it is one of the oldest Great Lakes lights. The original fuel was mineral oil and the beacon was a white light that flashed periodically. The lantern had serious problems with wind leaks, and many ship captains complained that the light would sometimes flicker and dim or go out completely. When operating properly, the light could be seen for nearly twenty miles from atop the eighty-foot bluff. A two-and-a-half-story duplex keeper's quarters with a full basement and partial attic was added in 1855.

Because of erosion on the bluff, a new light was constructed in the late 1800s, about a hundred feet inland from the original light. The eight-sided cast iron tower stood thirty-nine feet tall. This is the upper portion of the current lighthouse. Growing trees eventually reduced the visibility of the light, rendering it indis-

In 1881, Georgia Stebbins was appointed lighthouse keeper of North Point Light. One of her duties included winding the clockwork apparatus that rotated the light's lens every three hours.

North Point Lighthouse

tinguishable to seamen. Additional money was appropriated and in 1912 a new 35-foot base was built. The old tower was placed on a massive new base, 21.5 feet in diameter, bringing the height of the existing tower to 74 feet. North Point Light is approximately 160 feet above the lake level, making it still one of the tallest lights on the Great Lakes. Today the seam joining the two sections of this local landmark can plainly be seen. The light, which could be seen for twenty miles, was a fourth-order Fresnel lens manufactured by Barbier, Benard and Tiernne of Paris.

At one time North Point Lighthouse was alive with activity. For many years it also housed U.S. Coast Guard personnel and their families. Sadly, the light would later be abandoned, as it became less important. The tower contains many port hole windows, several of them appearing to be weeping rust colored tears. The lighthouse was darkened on March 15, 1994. The lens, light assembly, and clockwork mechanism have since been removed. The old keeper's quarters is in need of significant repair.

Current status: Inactive. Like many Wisconsin lighthouses, North Point is one whose long history is at a crossroads. The U.S. Coast Guard has declared this an excess property. No longer functional, its status is to be determined by government officials and interested parties including the Friends of Lake Park, a non-profit, volunteer group dedicated to the preservation and enjoyment of Milwaukee County's Lake Park, and by the Water Tower Landmark Trust. A lighthouse renovation and lease plan, submitted by the Friends, has been accepted by a Milwaukee County government committee. It is the intent of Milwaukee County, the Friends of Lake Park, and the Water Tower Landmark Trust and others to find a use for the lighthouse, keeper's dwelling, and surrounding grounds that is compatible with its parkland setting and historic nature. Estimates to convert the former lighthouse keeper's building into a maritime artifacts exhibit area and meeting facility for community groups approach $750,000. Limited public funds as well as monies from private foundations and public support to finance restoration efforts are being explored. Lake Park and the surrounding grounds are always open and you can get a great up-close look at the light just outside the fencing that surrounds the grounds. Immediately east of the light, a Wisconsin historical marker, dedicated in 1975, gives a brief history of the light. For further information contact the Water Tower Preservation Fund, Inc. P.O. Box 668, Milwaukee WI 53201.

How to get there: From I-43 near downtown Milwaukee exit at North Ave. Proceed east until North Ave. intersects Lake Drive; turn left (north) onto Lake Drive; go several blocks, past Bradford and Belleview. Lake Drive intersects with Wahl Ave. Turn right (south) onto Wahl; go approximately one block; the lighthouse is on your left in the park.

Milwaukee Breakwater Lighthouse

"Lighthouse tending isn't for sissies."

—U.S. Coast Guard boatswain's mate, stationed at the Milwaukee Breakwater Lighthouse.

Another of the "newer" Wisconsin lights, built in 1926, the Milwaukee Breakwater Lighthouse is one of the last examples on the Great Lakes of a fully enclosed breakwater lighthouse. Perched near the midpoint of a nearly four-mile-long, non-continuous breakwater, the Milwaukee Breakwater Lighthouse resembles a fortress. It has guided innumerable ships year-round safely into the main gap of the Milwaukee breakwater and harbor. The lighthouse consists of an enormous concrete slab base, a story and a half tall, a two-story white steel main house, and an additional two stories of steel tower topped by the black lantern and lens room, and various weather and communications antennas and other devices. The portholes and windows have glass that is a half-inch thick, which has been broken during wind and ice storms. The building itself is fifty-three feet tall and was initially painted red. Originally the lantern room had a fourth-order Fresnel lens, which at one time was used in the Milwaukee Pierhead Light, located to the west. Boaters sometimes tie up to the breakwater and fish from the cement pier.

During its manned years, Coast Guard personnel spent a rotational schedule of three days on and three days off at the light, year round. If radio communications to shore were cut off by bad weather, or the twenty-five-foot open Coast Guard lifeboat could not make the trip to the lighthouse for rotation of personnel, the men had to remain on duty until the weather broke. A minimum of two men called the lighthouse home with a crew of four the norm. Twelve hours on duty and an equal amount off constituted the typical lighthouse day.

In those days, radio beacons were used on Great Lakes vessels for navigation. Monitoring a transmitter at the station was one of the primary responsibilities of the crew, along with another important piece of equipment, the diaphone foghorn. It was difficult to get some shut-eye when the foghorn was in operation. Its loud moan, powered by monstrous air compressors, could be heard many miles out onto the big lake.

*I*n January of 1948 boatswain's mate, first class Michael Rotta recalled for a reporter, "You should have been here during the New Year's day snowstorm. The whole building shook from the waves that climbed up on the crib deck. The storm started about noon and by seven p.m. our communications to shore had been cut."

The lens room was cleaned every day, especially of the hundreds of spiders that took up residence along with their webs. Weather observations were logged four times daily. Cooking and cleaning were also routine chores.

The lighthouse had electricity and a black-and-white television provided by a local brewery. This modern convenience made the stay much more bearable. Playing cards and reading also helped pass the time.

A large gray door in the lower concrete base of the lighthouse opens to the inner harbor side where lighthouse service boats used to dock with Coast Guard personnel to exchange crews and replenish supplies. A hoist system helped in this difficult maneuver. In turbulent weather, a change of crew was not easily accomplished.

The Milwaukee Breakwater Lighthouse was automated in the 1960s.

Current status: Active aid to navigation. Red light flashes every 10 seconds; 61-foot focal plane, visible for 14 miles. Fog signal sounds two separate blasts every 20 seconds. The interior of the mighty light structure has been gutted.

How to get there: From downtown Milwaukee take I-794 East, exit at Plankinton Ave. On this ramp, proceed straight onto St. Paul Ave., 0.1 of a mile over the Milwaukee River bridge. Turn right (south) onto North Water St., proceed 0.4 mile to West Pittsburgh Ave. Turn left (east) onto Pittsburgh. Proceed 0.3 mile as this road winds and crosses the Milwaukee River, to a right (southeast) turn onto East Erie St. Proceed on Erie for 0.4 mile to a large parking lot where the Hoan Bridge will be visible on your left (east). Follow road left (east) along the harbor canal for 0.4 mile. The Milwaukee Pierhead Light will be directly in front of you and the Milwaukee Breakwater Lighthouse will be visible further east out in the harbor.

following page: Milwaukee Pierhead Light

Milwaukee Pierhead Light

Milwaukee has had a series of pier lights in its history marking several piers and breakwaters. The most notable is the Milwaukee Pierhead Light, a conical structure situated less than three-fourths of a mile west of the Milwaukee Breakwater Lighthouse. The Milwaukee Pierhead Light rests just east of the confluence of Milwaukee's three rivers, the Milwaukee, Menomonee, and Kinnickinnic. It marks the artificial channel dredged and completed in 1857 at a cost in excess of a half million dollars to replace the rivers' natural connection to Lake Michigan, which was one half-mile south of the present inlet. The original discharge of the rivers into the lake was closed and filled in about 1865. The red pierhead light guided schooners, sloops, barges, and, later, steamboats into the Milwaukee harbor.

Constructed in 1872 as an open-framework pierhead range tower, the Pierhead Light was rebuilt in 1906 as a conical steel-plated structure. The first light emitted was a fixed red beam from a fourth-order Fresnel lens within a circular lantern room. Later, a fifth-order Fresnel lens and a lantern room with ten sides replaced the original top. The tower stands forty-two feet tall and is typical of the red pierhead lights that dot Lake Michigan. After the Milwaukee Breakwater Light was built, the Pierhead Light was remotely controlled via an underwater cable.

This cylindrical light has been moved numerous times along the north pier as the Milwaukee lakefront underwent changes over the years. During World War II, a red brick building sat behind the light. Coast Guard accounts mention the frequent removal of vagrants who often found shelter around the lighthouse grounds. Currently the light is behind the Marcus Amphitheater and the south end of the Maier Festival Park (Summerfest grounds), immediately east of the Hoan Bridge. Adjacent to the light is a parking area and a popular fishing spot.

Current status: Active aid to navigation. The tower flashes a red light every four seconds; 45-foot focal plane, visible for 12 miles. No fog signal.

How to get there: From downtown Milwaukee take I-794 East, exit at Plankinton Ave. From this ramp, proceed straight onto St. Paul Ave., 0.1 of a mile over the Milwaukee River bridge. Turn right (south) onto North Water St., proceed 0.4 mile to West Pittsburgh Ave. Turn left (east) onto Pittsburgh. Proceed 0.3 mile as this road winds and crosses the Milwaukee River, to a right (southeast) turn onto East Erie St. Proceed on Erie for 0.4 mile to a large parking lot where the Hoan Bridge will be visible on your left (east). Follow road left (east) along the harbor canal for 0.4 mile. The lighthouse will be directly in front of you.

Racine

Racine owes its name to the many roots that once tangled the river. The early French fur traders named it *les racines*, "the roots." Appropriately, the mighty Root River joins Lake Michigan where Racine's harbor is today. Racine, founded in 1834 as Port Gilbert and incorporated in 1841, was an important port nestled along Lake Michigan's shoreline between Milwaukee and Chicago. The original harbor was too small and shallow for commercial shipping, so dredging took place to open the river mouth and harbor for maritime commerce that still thrives today. Racine has had lighthouses protecting her harbor for many years. Located at the mouth of the Root River, the town became a busy port in the nineteenth and twentieth centuries.

The Root River Lighthouse, also known as the old Government Lighthouse, was the first one built here in 1839. Located at the mouth of the Root River, the light was situated immediately east of Lake Ave. and 7th St. where the public library stands today. The conical Cream City brick light tower stood forty feet tall at the top of a sheer bluff, twenty feet from the lakeshore. The original light rotated, and was replaced by a fourth-order Fresnel lens in 1858. A keeper's quarters made of brick stood behind the lighthouse. The only father-and-son keeper team in Racine history, Martin and Edward W. Knudsen, served here. This lighthouse was removed from service in 1865. A new river mouth was dredged a half mile to the north of this lighthouse, ending its days of usefulness. The land and the lighthouse were sold by the State of Wisconsin in 1876 to an individual who demolished the lighthouse and outbuildings in order to construct his home.

In 1844 piers were built at the new mouth of the river and in 1849 a simple frame light was constructed at the end of the north pier. This light remained in service until 1859 when it was struck by the schooner *Neuman*, which carried the light away. Two piers that stretched out from the river mouth were built in 1861 and four years later the Racine Harbor Lighthouse was built two hundred feet from shore. The Harbor Lighthouse was lit for the first time on September 10, 1866. The light and keeper's quarters were constructed of brick.

In 1866 the fourth-order Fresnel lens from the Root River Light was placed in the Racine Harbor Lighthouse. Two years later the north pier was extended past the lighthouse and a second beacon with a red light was put into service. When sailors kept the red light to the left of the lighthouse, they were able to make safe harbor into Racine. A second building was later erected immediately west of the Racine Harbor Lighthouse to house the Life Saving Service. The light from the Harbor Lighthouse was eventually placed in the tower at the end of the north pier. The old tower was capped with a hip roof and the house was remodeled. Ultimately, the buildings were transformed into a U. S. Coast Guard Station.

Wind Point Lighthouse

Appropriately, there always seems to be a breeze blowing at Wind Point, which has also been called Racine Point and Windy Point. The lighthouse is a familiar area landmark and a much-used symbol of Racine. Prior to the building of the lighthouse, a lone, wind-blown tree on the point served as a landmark for Lake Michigan mariners.

This is a classic tower, one of the oldest and the third tallest lighthouse still operating on the Great Lakes. Built in 1880, north of the Racine Harbor, this light was originally put into service to warn mariners of the dangerous Racine Reef, nearly four miles southeast of Wind Point. Approximately a mile and one-quarter off the point in Lake Michigan are two other shoals both north and south of the lighthouse with depths less than twenty feet. The round tower is constructed of brick and iron. It stands 108 feet tall and has 144 iron steps to the top of the tower. The tower walls are a massive seven feet thick at the bottom. The tower is directly connected to the old keeper's house via a short walkway.

Seven keepers called the Wind Point Lighthouse home, including the first keeper, Mr. A. B. Finch. Normally the light was manned with a keeper, two assistants, and their families. The original light was a kerosene-fueled lamp that had to be refilled every eight hours. A third-order Fresnel lens displayed a flashing white light. A window below the lantern room flashed a red light that could be seen to the south to aid in marking the Racine Reef, which was signalized by a buoy. The red light could be seen only when mariners were in a straight course with the reef. A fog signal building with two brass foghorns was erected in 1900 and still faces the open lake. This vigorous warning could be heard as far away as ten miles, sounding three seconds out of every thirty seconds. The original Fresnel lens, now restored, is on display at the Wind Point Village Hall, which is the former keeper's dwelling. This lens contains twelve flash panels and rotated once every six

minutes to create a flash every thirty seconds. Electricity came to the light in 1924, only the second government light on the Great Lakes to become electrified. Automated in 1964, the tower uses a circling aerobeacon, a bulb of one thousand watts, and a reflector, producing a light visible for twenty-nine miles. The light is currently activated by photo cells and automatic timers. Following other improvements in technology, including ship radar, the foghorn was also dismantled in 1964. The former keeper's quarters are a white, two-story brick building with red roof boasting two chimneys and eight dormers.

The Wind Point Lighthouse story is an example of a light that has been taken over by a municipality with great success. For several years, the Village of Wind Point had leased the buildings and grounds from the Coast Guard. The lighthouse is on the National Register of Historic Places. A park-like setting affords a beautiful view of the lake. The surrounding grounds are well maintained and are open during daylight hours. The building currently is used for municipal services by the Wind Point Police Department and Village Hall as well as a residence for the caretaker. Today the Village of Wind Point owns the property while the Coast Guard still maintains the beacon. Recently, a non-profit friends group has formed. Its mission is to preserve the lighthouse through education. For further information write to: Friends of Wind Point Lighthouse, Suite 200, 601 Lake Ave., Racine WI 53401; or phone (262) 639-2026.

One of the worst storms on Lake Michigan occurred on October 16, 1880, shortly after Wind Point Lighthouse was put into service. More than a thousand craft were snared in the lake's turbulence and fought to find safe harbor. The largest number of ships were off the Wisconsin shore and the light from Wind Point helped many of them to safety in Racine and Kenosha's harbors.

Current status: Active aid to navigation. White light rotates and flashes every 20 seconds, 111 foot focal plane, visible for 29 miles. No fog signal. The lighthouse grounds are open from 6 a.m. to 11 p.m. daily.

How to get there: From I-94 take the 7 Mile Road (exit 326) east. Proceed approx. 5.9 miles to Hwy 32. Go right (south) on Hwy. 32 approx. 3.4 miles to 4 Mile Road. Turn left (east) onto 4 Mile Road. 4 Mile Road will become County G for approx. 0.75 mile. Continue going east past where Cty G turns to the right. Continue going straight (east). The road will curve to the right and become Lighthouse Drive. Proceed less than 0.25 mile, watch for a sign for the Wind Point Police Department and Village Hall on your left. Turn left (east) and proceed one block to a parking area near the light.

preceding page: Wind Point Lighthouse

Racine Reef Lighthouse

According to Native American legend, this reef was once an island with trees. In a twenty-year span in the late 1800s, nearly a dozen ships struck the submerged reef and were sunk. The reef, a treacherous limestone rock outcropping, is located more than two miles east of Racine harbor, in Lake Michigan.

This was a most difficult light to construct, since it was located on a limestone reef, one and a half miles long and three-quarters of a mile wide. The water depth was less than twenty feet, and as little as seven feet in places.

110

courtesy Al Krescanko

Racine Reef Light, dismantled in 1961

Construction began in 1905 and the station became known as Racine's Ellis Island or Statute of Liberty. The sixty-foot tower had a fourth-order Fresnel lens that displayed a flashing red light visible for nearly twenty miles on a clear night. The base alone was seventy-five feet square and rose twenty feet out of the water. The building was constructed of white and brown brick covering an iron skeleton. It was described as a Victorian home, four to five stories tall. An American flag flew proudly from the highest point of the light. The lighthouse tender, *Hyacinth*, assisted in the building of the Reef Lighthouse and also delivered coal to this station.

Modern Racine Reef Light

Coast Guard personnel manned the light station in typical shifts of four days on duty followed by two or three days off, when weather permitted them to reach shore! This job was said to be one of the most difficult on the Great Lakes. During exceptionally bad winters, crewmen were marooned on Racine Reef for up to twenty-four days, locked in by ice as high as twenty-five feet. For this reason, enough supplies for a month were always kept stocked. This was one of a handful of lighthouses to remain in operation year round. In 1928 the Reef Light won a government award for being the neatest of all Lake Michigan lights. This light station also featured a compressed air fog signal that caused the light to vibrate quite vigorously. Perch fishing and swimming were pleasant activities for crewmen. They also enjoyed a friendly greeting from passing pleasure boats. The light was taken out of service in 1954 and dismantled in 1961. Even today, Racine residents lament the destruction of this unique light.

Current status: The present, modern, skeletal Racine Reef tower light stands 45 feet tall. A white light flashes every six seconds, visible for 12 miles. Fog signal sounds a two-second blast every 15 seconds.

How to get there: From I-94 take the Highway 20 east exit. Hwy. 20 becomes Washington Ave. Stay on Washington until you see signs for Hwy. 32. Turn left (north) on Hwy. 32. Go approx. 3 blocks to 4th St. (which is also called Christopher Columbus Causeway). Turn right (east) on Columbus and follow signs to the Reefpoint Marina. Continue through the marina to the farthest parking lot to the north. The light is located two miles due East of the harbor. Good views of the light are possible from the walkways along the lake and the two-story elevated overlook in the marina.

Racine North Breakwater Light (Old Red Lighthouse)

Breakwater lights have been a part of the Racine harbor since the middle 1800s. This old red light was constructed in 1910 on the newly built north breakwater. The rather odd looking red, spidery, open-framed structural tower stands fifty-three feet tall and had a sixth-order Fresnel lens that exhibited a red light. The tower is covered with metal plating and has porthole windows. The keeper gained access to the tower via an exterior stairway to the first level and then ladders inside to the lantern room. In addition to the light, this tower also had two fog signal horns.

Today, the light is no longer used as a navigational aid. "Big Red," as the light is known to locals, is the focal point of the modern-day Racine Reefpoint Marina and is illuminated at night. However, the fate of this light was once in jeopardy. In 1987 the Coast Guard determined the old light to have outgrown its usefulness. Proposed destruction of the structure caused a public outcry that ultimately led to its rescue. One of the few remaining lights of its kind on the Great Lakes, it is perched atop a concrete and boulder breakwater.

112

Current status: Ornamental use only.

How to get there: From I-94 take the Highway 20 east exit. Hwy. 20 becomes Washington Ave. Stay on Washington until you see signs for Hwy. 32. Turn left (north) on Hwy. 32. Go approx. three blocks to 4th St. (which is also called Christopher Columbus Causeway). Turn right (east) on Columbus and follow signs to the Reefpoint Marina. Continue through the marina to the farthest parking lot to the north. Good views of the light are possible from the walkways along the Lake and the two-story elevated overlook in the marina. The tall tower of Wind Point Lighthouse, 3.25 miles to the north, may also be seen in the distance.

Racine North Breakwater Light

Kenosha

Like many Wisconsin cities, the settlement and development of Kenosha was directly connected to its harbor and Lake Michigan. Kenosha's strategic location on the lake between Milwaukee and Chicago and its natural harbor were a draw for ships carrying both immigrants and goods. The city was first known as Pike or Pike Creek, and then later changed to Southport in 1837 as the harbor gained more importance. The current name Kenosha is derived from the Native American word for pike, *kenozia*, which inhabited the waters of a large creek nearby.

In the 1830s, before more permanent structures were built, the first "lighthouse" in this area was no more elaborate than a ten-foot oak tree stump with a wood fire atop. Next came a four-posted, two-story sash lantern. Its sixty-dollar cost was financed directly by local citizens. A wooden pierhead light later existed at the Kenosha harbor and was at the mercy of Lake Michigan's fury and vessels navigating its waters. Many a ship had a run-in with the lighthouse. For example, on November 20, 1892, the schooner *Evaline* collided with the pierhead lighthouse, causing considerable damage. At that time a breakwater had not yet been built. A long catwalk connected the lighthouse to the eastern end of the north pier. Early in the 1900s a 1,040-foot steel catwalk, the first on Lake Michigan, led the keeper safely to the pierhead light. This catwalk would later be introduced at many other government lighthouses on Lake Michigan because of its inaugural success at Kenosha.

Kenosha North Pierhead Light at dusk

Kenosha North Pierhead Light

Harbor improvements were initiated in 1899 and completed several years later. Included were a longer north pier, a detached breakwater, and a newly remodeled pier lighthouse. A more powerful and considerably louder compressed air fog signal was also part of the upgrade. Kenosha again was at the forefront, being one of the initial places where the new fog equipment was tested. Kenosha rightly boasted that after these enhancements, it was the best equipped harbor of refuge on Lake Michigan.

Another typical Lake Michigan red pierhead light, the current Kenosha beacon, was built in 1906, replacing the older wooden structure. It stands at the entrance to the Port of Kenosha, located at the end of the 750-foot concrete and steel-reinforced north pier. Originally, a fourth-order Fresnel lens graced the tower. Currently an automated modern beacon sits inside the crosshatched glass black lantern room and provides the light. Electricity runs through a cable for the length of the pier. Remarkably, a pint-sized 250-watt bulb supplies the illumination. The tower stands fifty feet tall and consists of a dozen tiers of metal riveted plates. A battery-powered auxiliary light that rested outside the lantern room has since been removed. The portholes used years ago by the lightkeepers to monitor outdoor weather conditions still dot the tower.

Current status: Active aid to navigation. A red isophase light cycles three seconds on, three seconds off, with a 50-foot focal plane, visible for 12 miles. Fog signal sounds a three-second blast in a 30-second span and is operated seasonally from April to December. The tower is not open to the public. For more information contact the Kenosha County Historical Society, 6300 Third Ave., Kenosha, WI 53143. Phone (262) 654-5770.

How to get there: From I-94 go east on Hwy 158 (exit 342) approximately 6.7 miles to Sheridan Road. As you enter the city limits this highway will change names to 52nd St. Turn left (north) on Sheridan Road. Travel 0.2 of a mile to 50th St. (also called Lighthouse Drive). Turn right (east) on 50th St. and proceed 0.3 of a mile to Simmons Island. Turn right and go past the U. S. Coast Guard Station (which will be on your right) and the Old Southport Lighthouse (on your left). You will see the Kenosha Yacht Club straight ahead; the road curves to the left. Follow this road until it ends in a public parking lot. The lighthouse stands on the end of the north pier. Immediately north of the light is a public beach where you may enjoy a pleasant stroll.

Old Southport (Kenosha) Lighthouse

In the late 1830s Kenosha was known as Southport, being the southernmost port in Wisconsin. There has been a government lighthouse here since the first light was built on Simmons Island in 1848. Fitted with the oil-fueled Winslow Lewis lighting system, and an Argand lamp with a silver parabolic reflector, the beacon sat in an octagonal lantern room. In 1858, a little-known second lighthouse replaced the initial light and the outmoded Argand lamp gave way to a fifth-order Fresnel lens.

Deterioration of the second light due to an unstable foundation and the need for extensive repairs necessitated a third and completely new Southport Lighthouse. The light that stands today was built in 1866. The date is clearly inscribed above the decorative tower doors. Southport Light stands fifty-five feet tall, with a focal plane above the lake of seventy-four feet. The round tower was constructed of Milwaukee Cream City brick, a very durable masonry product common to southeastern Wisconsin. A fourth-order Fresnel lens and a fixed white light punctuated with flashes originally was the light's signature. Later, a white flashing light was employed. Kerosene fueled the beacon that could be seen on Lake Michigan for a maximum of fourteen nautical miles.

Listed on the National and State of Wisconsin Register of Historic Places, Southport Light is located on Simmons Island, adjacent to Simmons Island Park, overlooking Lake Michigan. It was a meaningful beacon, the first in Wisconsin north of the major port of Chicago. The keeper's quarters, often called "the cottage," was constructed in 1867, a few dozen steps from the tower. Southport Light was manned until 1940, but the building continued to house the keeper and his family who remained to tend the harbor pierhead light.

Old Southport Light was given some stiff competition in 1880 when the Wind Point Lighthouse was built to the north in Racine County. Wind Point was taller and sported a stronger Fresnel lens than Southport. Plans called for the discontinuation of Southport's beacon in the late 1880s. The light was not removed from service, however, until the spring of 1906 when the Kenosha North Pierhead Light was inaugurated, marking the entrance to Kenosha's harbor. Old Southport then remained dark for ninety years. Taller lights, which could be observed at a greater distance out on Lake Michigan, Grosse Point Light in Evanston, Illinois, and Wind Point Light in Racine, lessened Southport's significance. A tripod weather signal mast, twenty-five feet high, displaying storm warning lights and flags, replaced the lantern room in 1913 and functioned in that capacity for nearly half a century. A sign above the door to the tower entrance read "U.S. Weather Bureau Storm Warning Tower." Sadly, the tower was mothballed in the 1960s.

At one point the venerable structure was going to be demolished. Local people refused to let the Southport light die, however. Preservation efforts led by several interested lighthouse buffs slowly took hold and new life was breathed into the old light. The National Park Service, the Kenosha County Historical Society, the State Historical Society of Wisconsin, and private grants provided funding for the Southport Lighthouse restoration. Finally, in 1994, a replica of the original ten-sided black lantern room adorned the tower gallery deck. A new, modern 300-millimeter plastic lens was installed, featuring a white, 200-watt, high-intensity light. As the country celebrated its independence on the Fourth of July 1996, the Old Southport Light was lit once again and celebrated its own independence. The light does not function as a navigational aid, but is lit to celebrate anniversaries, birthdays, memorials, and other special occasions. To light the Southport Light, call the Kenosha Historical Society at (262) 654-5770. It is hoped that interested people will eventually be able to climb the circular seventy-two-step wrought iron stairway to the lantern room to view Lake Michigan and downtown Kenosha. Additional plans include restoration of the keeper's cottage with the hope of refurbishing it as a future maritime museum. The Old Southport Light will have come full circle.

Southport Light had several notable women tending it. The only woman keeper at the light, Lorinda Merrill, was appointed in 1871 at age 63 after the death of her husband, Joseph. She served with distinction for one year. Their teenage daughter Emma was also the assistant keeper to both her mother and father at Southport. Emma is buried in Kenosha's Green Ridge cemetery, a lighthouse engraved on her tombstone. Another woman, Mary DeDiemer, served as an assistant keeper for nearly three decades.

Old Southport (Kenosha) Lighthouse

Tombstone of Emma Merrill, assistant keeper, Southport Light

118

*"I have so many fond memories of my childhood. I dream of going back to that lighthouse a lot . . .
in my dreams, it always looks the same as when I was a little girl."*

—Lillian Bennett O'Neil, daughter of assistant keeper Fred Bennett, recalling her days
at Southport Light, circa 1916. She and her playmates had a playhouse in the Southport tower.

Current status: The lantern is lit only for special occasions. Refurbishing work continues on the lighthouse and keeper's quarters. The lighthouse property is open to the public and owned by the City of Kenosha. Fundraising efforts include an annual Door County-style fish boil in the fall at the nearby Kenosha Yacht Club. For further information contact the Kenosha County Historical Society, 6300 Third Ave., Kenosha , WI. 53143.

How to get there: From I-94 go east on Hwy 158 (exit 342) approximately 6.7 miles to Sheridan Road. As you enter the city limits this highway changes names to 52nd St. Turn left (north) on Sheridan Road. Travel 0.2 of a mile to 50th St., (also called Lighthouse Drive). Turn right (east) on 50th St. and proceed 0.3 of a mile to Simmons Island. Turn right. The U. S. Coast Guard Station will be on your right, the Old Southport Lighthouse on your left.

Cana Island lantern

Lighting The Way For The Future

A romantic era in Wisconsin has passed into history. Sadly, the position of lightkeeper is obsolete and will not be found today on anyone's resume. The days of the manned lighthouse are gone forever. Lighthouses stand as symbols of a bygone era, a time that was simpler but, in many ways, more challenging and dangerous. Scientific and technological advances in the twentieth century have reduced the significance of many of these treasured guardians of navigation to lonely landmarks. Once proud lights have given way to highly efficient but cold, impersonal beacons. Devoted keepers have been replaced by timers and photo cells. The efficient cost-saving structures of today certainly lack the charm of their predecessors.

People are nostalgic about lighthouses. These sentinels continue to have historic as well as scenic and cultural significance. They invite us to go back in time. Wisconsin's lighthouses have procured a critical place and are indelibly linked with the history of the state through their considerable services to mariners. Years ago, hundreds of courageous men, women, and families faithfully carried out their sometimes lonely and dangerous duties watching over the lights. Countless seafarers have these keepers to thank for their loyalty. These staunch beacons of safety are a conduit, a porthole to Wisconsin's past. It is difficult to imagine the Badger State without them.

Due to budget-cutting measures, today's remaining lighthouses are at the mercy of the elements and are vulnerable to deterioration and vandalism. Some of these beams of life are slowly dying. In most cases, the Coast Guard is in charge of maintaining only the lights themselves, not the buildings or surrounding grounds. Many lighthouses are no longer the proud beacons they once were. Some are in dire need of human intervention to save them from becoming only symbols of the past. We were surprised and dismayed at the number of lights we visited which had fallen on hard times. Several of them had significant graffiti and were in various stages of ruin, and some lighthouse grounds were overgrown.

The need for public action to preserve remaining lighthouses is compelling. As these guiding lights fall into disrepair or are demolished, a part of our heritage is forever lost. It is not wise to ignore the historical significance of many of these old Wisconsin lights.

Lighthouses possess great potential to be renovated and converted for new uses. Nationally, lighthouses have been successfully transformed into museums, parks, bed and breakfasts, conference and nature centers, and educational and recreational facilities, or have become part of various park systems. The State of Wisconsin has been approached about developing a plan for the preservation, maintenance, and management of a number of lights. It is costly to maintain existing lighthouses. Funding is critical to insure their future viability.

Fortunately, in some cases, the automation, abandonment and mothballing of many of our majestic lighthouses has actually allowed the general public to view and learn more of their stories than otherwise would have been possible. More lighthouses than ever before have and will continue to be turned into living history museums that offer tours and a glimpse back in time. Restored lighthouses not only provide educational opportunities but also can generate revenue as tourist attractions for progressive communities. Admission fees often provide needed funds for lighthouse upkeep.

Success stories of lighthouse preservation efforts in Wisconsin include the Apostle Islands, Grassy Island Range Lights, Chambers Island, Eagle Bluff, Pottawatomie, Baileys Harbor Range Lights, Two Rivers North Pier, Old Port Washington, North Point, Wind Point, Racine North Breakwater, and Southport (Kenosha) Light. Discussions are currently underway to determine the future of several other beacons. The National Parks Service, historical societies, museums, private citizens, governmental agencies, and friends groups have all played vital roles in lighthouse preservation and restoration in Wisconsin. Many of these lights are the ones that are open to the public. Leasing lights from the Coast Guard has worked well in several instances. The State Historical Society of Wisconsin is also involved in lighthouse preservation efforts.

The spirit of lighthouses is expressed well in a United States Lighthouse Board Report from 1868: "Nothing indicates the liberality, prosperity, or intelligence of a nation more clearly than the facilities which it affords for the safe approach of the mariner to its shores."

120

Not surprising, there is remarkable local support for any number of Wisconsin lights designated as surplus property. Wisconsin is known for its stewardship. The number of people involved in lighthouse preservation and restoration is growing. It has been the tireless grass-roots efforts of these dedicated local residents that make possible the survival of many of these lights. Without their endless hours of unselfish dedication to the cause of lighthouse conservation, many of these beacons would be in serious jeopardy of losing the battle against time and the elements. Preserved and renovated lighthouses are a tribute to the determination of these citizens. The fate of smaller, more remote and inaccessible, "less important" lights, those that may not be as well suited to changing uses, is not as obvious. Location does have its advantages.

Clearly, a good many lights still provide security to an untold number of people. The primary function of lighthouses remains unchanged. They continue to be valuable, functional aids to navigation, although primarily for smaller, recreational pleasure craft. Modern cargo-carrying vessels have technologically advanced equipment, including sophisticated satellite technology, to determine their exact positions precisely and guide their way safely.

The "For Sale" sign may not be visible at any Wisconsin lighthouses, but the fate of many will be determined by the federal government's desire to dispose of some of these excess or surplus properties. The United States Coast Guard continues to operate more than a hundred Great Lakes lighthouses, but is removing itself from the business of lighthouse building maintenance. The Guard is extremely interested in partnering with those committed to lighthouse preservation. Their "Partnering to Preserve" program actively seeks to turn over lighthouses permanently to entities that are able and willing to preserve and maintain them. Considerable debate continues as to the best ways to transfer responsibility of lighthouses. Costs associated with lighthouse upkeep are high. With limited tax subsidies, other sources of funding are necessary if they are to survive. The Coast Guard continues to maintain many of the lights that currently serve as navigational aids, but their resources are dwindling.

Interest in lighthouses appears to be at an all time high. Everyone seems to know about them and many people have a favorite, perhaps one they have visited or have only read about. It could even be a lighthouse remembered from childhood. Lighthouse images are seen everywhere today. Witness the innumerable lighthouse items available in gift shops and catalogs. There are even gift shops devoted exclusively to lighthouses. They are symbols for businesses and churches, subjects for countless artists. Great Lakes lights have been featured on U.S. postage stamps, in print media, and on television. There are even lighthouse trading cards.

In Wisconsin, approximately thirty-three of these grand structures continue to function, still serving their original purpose, signaling vessels to safe port. They add to the enchantment of Wisconsin's coastlines and provide unique opportunities for lighthouse enthusiasts, artists, and photographers. Many of the lighthouses chronicled here are more than a century old and have performed a vital role in commerce and sea trade.

"May the wind and the wave
Be your friend
May you stand the storm
and the hand of the Lord
Bring you safely to
harbor again"

—Author unknown

⚓

Wisconsin's motto is "Forward." As the Badger State enters a new century and a new millennium, it is our hope that the essence of these lights and the dedication that their keepers exhibited will encourage people to preserve as much of this rich maritime heritage as possible. Lighthouses speak to vigilance. Scores of Wisconsinites have been relentless in their efforts to safeguard many lights. In some small way we hope our venture to showcase these lights through our photography, and a bit of their interesting history, will help prevent this nautical symbol from eventually vanishing. We trust that numerous lighthouses will continue to be able to "leave the light on" and illuminate our way. Lighthouse preservation is worth the effort. Let us all strive to keep these legends alive and their lights burning.

121

Sturgeon Bay Canal North Pierhead Light

Milwaukee Pierhead Light

Lighthouse Organizations and Restoration Efforts

If you have an interest in lighthouses and their history, you are encouraged to join any of the following groups. There is no shortage of organizations or ways you can become involved.

Great Lakes Lighthouse Keepers Association (GLLKA)

The Great Lakes Lighthouse Keepers Association is a non-profit organization incorporated in 1983. Its purpose is to facilitate the accumulation and exchange of information about the histories of lighthouses and their keepers so that life at these stations may be accurately interpreted and their history preserved. GLLKA is dedicated to the development of a new generation of lighthouse preservationists. Young people are encouraged to participate in Association activities. Members meet at annual conferences near different light stations to share information about lighthouses, discuss and illustrate restoration projects in their area, seek ways to address issues of common concern, and visit area lights. Cruises are periodically arranged to view offshore lighthouse sites. Additionally, GLLKA works with other lighthouse organizations to share preservation techniques and provide a network for interested volunteers. The Association also produces a quarterly publication, The Beacon. It features articles, photos, and artwork to inform members of events and other Great Lakes lighthouse news. Members can also exchange information through the newsletter. It is an invaluable publication for the lighthouse researcher.

The Association invites you to become a member. GLLKA is a means for historians, keepers, descendants, artists, teachers, photographers and all others interested in the history and continuing concerns of Great Lakes lighthouses to further explore and preserve this unique maritime heritage.

> Great Lakes Lighthouse Keepers Association
> c/o Henry Ford Estate
> 4901 Evergreen Road
> Dearborn, MI 48128
> (313) 436-9150
> www.gllka.com

U.S. Lighthouse Society

Wayne Wheeler founded the Society, a historical and educational organization, during the 1983-1984 period. Its purpose is to educate, inform, and entertain those who are interested in America's lighthouses and lightships, past and present. Lighthouses are unique historical and architectural structures and important elements of our maritime heritage. New uses must be developed to preserve those structures for future generations. The U.S. Lighthouse Society is the hub of communication between various lighthouse groups. It achieves this by distributing information through a quarterly magazine, The Keeper's Log, and providing information as requested.

> United States Lighthouse Society
> President and Founder, Wayne Wheeler
> 244 Kearny St., 5th Floor
> San Francisco, CA 94108
> (415) 362-7255

The Lighthouse Preservation Society

The Lighthouse Preservation Society is a non-profit organization that has made lighthouse preservation a national issue. Its mission is to preserve historic lighthouse structures for future generations, to open them up to public use and enjoyment, and to document their history and that of their keepers. Congressional hearings, conferences, the sponsorship of National Lighthouse Day and its celebrations, the nomination of ten U.S. lighthouse postage stamps, and the

raising of nearly $6 million for over 160 lighthouse projects are some of the Society's accomplishments.
Ongoing goals include: Preservation of America's 800 + remaining lighthouses
Development of museums, recreational and other uses of lighthouses
Increase of public awareness of the plight and potential of lighthouses
Interpretation and documentation of lighthouse technology and history

The Lighthouse Preservation Society
4 Middle St.
Suite 226/225
Newburyport, MA 01950
(800) 727-BEAM (2326)

Lighthouse Digest

Lighthouse Digest is the world's only monthly lighthouse magazine. Each issue contains current lighthouse news and historical stories, the Doomsday List of endangered lighthouses, a calendar of events of lighthouse activities around the country including boat tours and open houses, and new lighthouse products on the market.

The American Lighthouse Foundation

The American Lighthouse Foundation is a non-profit organization, dedicated to saving lighthouses, their history, and their heritage. The foundation has recently restored several East Coast lights and is in the process of restoring others. For information, call 1-800-668-7737.
Lighthouse Depot is "the most complete selection of lighthouse memorabilia ever assembled." You may order on-line at www.lighthousedepot.com or call 1-800-758-1444.

124

Lighthouse Digest, The American Lighthouse Foundation, and Lighthouse Depot
P.O. Box 1690
U.S. Route 1
Wells, ME 04090
(800) 668-7737
www.lighthousedigest.com

State Historical Society of Wisconsin (SHSW)

The SHSW is involved with preservation efforts for many of Wisconsin's lighthouses. For further information, contact:

Richard A. Bernstein, Historian
Division of Historic Preservation
State Historical Society of Wisconsin
816 State Street
Madison, WI 53706-1488
(608) 264-6500
E-mail: rabernstein@mail.shsw.wisc.edu

modern lens
Michigan Island Light tower, Apostle Islands

Wisconsin Lighthouse Summary

LIGHT NAME	ACTIVE ?	BUILT	HT (FT)	LENS TYPE	VIEWING	TOURS
WISCONSIN POINT	YES	1913	42	MODERN	X	
SAND ISLAND	YES	1881	44	MODERN	X (B)	X (S)
RASPBERRY ISLAND	NO (M)	1863	45	MODERN	X (B)	X (S)
DEVILS ISLAND	YES	1897	82	FRESNEL (N) & MODERN	X (B)	X (S)
OUTER ISLAND	YES	1874	90	MODERN	X (B)	X (S)
MICHIGAN ISL. OLD	NO	1857	64	————	X (B)	X (S)
MICHIGAN ISL. NEW	YES	1929	112	MODERN	X (B)	X (S)
LA POINTE	YES	1895	67	MODERN	X (B)	
CHEQUAMEGON	NO (M)	1895	42	MODERN	X (B)	
ASHLAND	YES	1915	60	MODERN	X	
NEENAH	YES	1945	40	MODERN	X	
ASYLUM BAY	NO	1940	42	————	X	
ROCKWELL	YES	1909	42	MODERN	PRIVATE	
FOND DU LAC	YES	1933	56	MODERN	X	
MENOMINEE	YES	1927	25	MODERN	X	
GREEN ISLAND RUINS	NO (M)	1863	40	MODERN	RUINS (B)	
PESHTIGO REEF	YES	1934	72	MODERN	X (B)	
GREEN BAY ENTR.	YES	1935	72	FRESNEL	X (B)	
LONG TAIL PT. RUINS	NO	1848	85	————	RUINS (B)	
GRASSY ISL. RANGE	NO (R)	1872	35 & 25	————	X	
SHERWOOD POINT	YES	1883	35	FRESNEL	PRIVATE	X (D)
CHAMBERS ISL.	NO (M)	1868	42	MODERN	X (B)	X (D)
EAGLE BLUFF	YES	1868	43	FRESNEL (N) & MODERN	X	X
POTTAWATOMIE	NO (M)	1858	41	MODERN	X (B)	X (D)
PLUM RANGE LTS.	YES	1896 & 1965	65 & 40	FRESNEL & MODERN	X (B)	X (D)
PILOT ISLAND	YES	1858	46	MODERN	X (B)	X (D)
CANA ISLAND	YES	1869	86	FRESNEL	X	X
OLD BAILEYS	NO	1852	40	————	X	
BAILEYS RANGE LTS.	NO (M)	1869	35 & 21	MODERN	X	X (D)
STURG. BAY BRK.	YES	1903	43	MODERN	X	X (D)
STURG. BAY CANAL	YES	1903	98	FRESNEL	X	X (D)
ALGOMA	YES	1932	42	FRESNEL	X	
KEWAUNEE	YES	1931	43	FRESNEL	X	
RAWLEY POINT	YES	1893	111	MODERN	X	
TWO RIVERS	NO	1886	36	DECORATIVE	X	X (G)
MANITOWOC	YES	1918	50	FRESNEL	X	
SHEBOYGAN	YES	1915	50	MODERN	X	
PORT WASH. OLD	NO (R)	1860	50	————	X	
PORT WASH. BRK.	YES	1935	78	MODERN	X	
KEVICH	YES	1981	45	MODERN	PRIVATE	
NORTH POINT	NO	1912	74	————	X	
MILW. BRK.	YES	1926	53	MODERN	X	
MILW. PIER.	YES	1906	42	MODERN	X	
WIND POINT	YES	1880	108	MODERN	X	
RACINE REEF	NO (M)	1905	60	MODERN	REMOVED	
RACINE NORTH BRK.	NO	1910	53	————	X	
KENOSHA PIER.	YES	1906	50	MODERN	X	
SOUTHPORT	YES (C)	1866	55	MODERN	X	

LEGEND: M=MODERN METAL TOWER OR POLE
S=SEASONALLY
R=BEING RESTORED
B=BY BOAT
D=DOOR CO. LIGHTHOUSE WALK
G=SELF GUIDED
C=CEREMONIAL (NOT USED FOR NAVIGATION)
N=NOT USED

About the Photography

The majority of the photographs in this book were taken during the last two years. All color images were recorded on 35 mm slide film. We use Nikon equipment and our favorite lenses are two zooms, a 70-210 mm and a 28-85 mm. Whenever possible we use a tripod, a Bogen 3221 with a 3055 ball head, and a cable release. Our film of choice is Fujichrome Velvia (ISO 50) rated at ISO 40. Its crisp, non-grainy, color-saturated images are tough to beat. When a tripod is not practical and we must hand-hold the camera, such as on several of our boat excursions, we use several Ektachrome films for a little faster speed while still getting good color. We rarely use filters with the exception of an occasional polarizer to enhance a blue sky if necessary.

If you have an interest in any of the photographs as prints, please contact us.

126

Wind Point Lighthouse, Racine

Bibliography

Adamson, Hans Christian. *Keeper of the Lights.* Greenberg Publisher. 1955.

Algoma Record-Herald, Volume 106, Number 2.

Anchor News. Manitowoc Maritime Museum. March 1978.

Anderson, Harriet J., and Mary Dana Pawlitzke. *The Two Rivers Story.* The Centennial Committee 1978.

Apostle Islands Newsletter. 1998.

Around the Archipelago: Apostle Islands National Lakeshore. Volume 12, Number 1, 1997-1998.

Around the Archipelago: Apostle Islands National Lakeshore. Volume 13, Number 1, 1998-1999.

Asplund, Arvid. *The Story of Rogers Street*. 1986.

Badke, Frances. *Eagle Lighthouse.* Door Co. Publishing Co. Sturgeon Bay, WI. 1994.

Beacon Index. Great Lakes Lighthouse Keepers Association. Vol. 1 through 15. 1998.

Blackwell, Bob. "Lighthouse Life's Loud, Lonely" *Milwaukee Sentinel*. December 24, 1962.

Brockhoff, Beth. "Keeping the Lighthouse on Chambers Island." *The Herald-Leader*. Menominee, MI.-Marinette, WI. October 25, 1988.

Browne, Lewis. "Reef Light Two Miles From City Little Known to Racine Residents." *The Racine Review*. May 10, 1929.

Buchen, Gustave W. *Historic Sheboygan County*. 1944.

Caesar, Pete. *Let There Be Light.* Ocean and Great Lakes Marine Press. USA. 1984.

Caesar, Pete. *Let There Be Light II*. Ocean and Great Lakes Marine Press. USA. 1993.

Charles, Craig. *Exploring Door County*. NorthWord Press, Inc. Minocqua, WI. 1990.

Chase, Mary Ellen. *The Story of Lighthouses.* Norton and Company. 1965.

Clifford, Mary Louise, and J. Candace. *Women Who Kept The Lights (An Illustrated History of Female Lighthouse Keepers)*. 1993.

Conner, John. "Life on the Light." *Green Bay Press-Gazette*. April 9, 1974.

Cooper, David, et al. *The Development of Maritime Industries and Lake Shipping in the Apostle Islands: 1990 Underwater Archeological Investigations in the Apostle Islands.* State Historical Society of Wisconsin. 1991.

Davenport, Don. *Fire and Ice: Shipwreck on Lake Michigan*. Northword Press. 1983.

Devlin, Sean P. "Old Racine Lighthouse Historic Site?" *Racine Journal Times*. September 29, 1974.

Dunwiddie, William E. *The Parks of Neenah.* 1993.

"Entrance To Harbor Here Well Lighted." *The Green Bay Press-Gazette*. July 18, 1934.

Feret, Lori. "The North Shore to Duluth." *The Beacon*. Great Lakes Lighthouse Keepers Association. Vol. 15, No. 2, 1997.

"Fishing Village Beams With Maritime History." *Herald-Times Reporter*. Manitowoc-Two Rivers, WI. May 31, 1981.

"Foghorn House Restoration Sought." *Racine Journal Times*. April 4, 1992.

Glaman, Richard. "Inner Harbor Lighthouse Called Home by 'Wickies'." *Milwaukee Sentinel*. November 23, 1961.

The Great Lakes. An Environmental Atlas and Resource Book. The United States Environmental Protection Agency and the Government of Canada. 1995.

Guide to Door County Lighthouses. Eagle Bluff Lighthouse Committee of the Door County Historical Society.

Gutsche, Andrea, Barbara Chisholm, and Russel Floren. *Alone In The Night: Lighthouses of the Georgian Bay, Manitoulin Island and the North Channel*. 1996.

Harrison, Timothy. "A Brief History of Rawley Point (Twin River Point) Lighthouse." *Lighthouse Digest*. February, 1996. Vol. V, No. 2.

Held, Tom. "County Backs Preservationists' Plan for Lake Park Lighthouse." *Milwaukee Journal Sentinel*. February 10, 1999.

Historic Milwaukee Lightship Gives Place to Modern Devices. July 22, 1927. Historic Preservation Institute of the University of Wisconsin-Milwaukee.

Hemming, Robert J. *Gales of November: The Sinking of the Edmund Fitzgerald*. 1981.

History of Kimberly Point Lighthouse. Neenah, Wisconsin Park and Recreation Department.

History of the Kenosha (Southport) Lighthouse. Kenosha County Historical Society.

Holland, Francis Ross, Jr. *America's Lighthouses: Their Illustrated History since 1716*. The Stephen Green Press. 1972.

Holland, F. Ross. *Lighthouses*. Barnes and Noble, Inc., Michael Friedman Publishing Group, Inc. 1997.

Holland, H.R. *Old Peninsula Days*. Heartland Press. Minocqua, WI. 1990.

Holland, H.R. *History of Door County*. 1917.

Hyde, Charles K. *The Northern Lights: Lighthouses of the Upper Great Lakes*. Wayne State University Press. 1995.

Instructions to Light Keepers & Masters of Light House Vessels. Great Lakes Lightkeepers Association. 1989.

Janda, Louie and Rosie. *Cana Island Memories*. Great Lakes Lighthouse Keepers Association. Vol. 14, No. 2. 1996.

Karges, Steven. "Baileys Harbor Range Lights." Door County Maritime Museum Lighthouse Walk. 1998.

Karges, Steven. "Cana Island Light." Door County Maritime Museum Lighthouse Walk. 1998.

Karges, Steven. "Chambers Island Light." Door County Maritime Museum Lighthouse Walk. 1998

Karges, Steven. "Eagle Bluff Light." Door County Maritime Museum Lighthouse Walk. 1998.

Karges, Steven. "Plum Island Range Lights." Door County Maritime Museum Lighthouse Walk. 1998.

Karges, Steven. "Pilot Island Light." Door County Maritime Museum Lighthouse Walk. 1998.

Karges, Steven. "Pottawatomie Light—Rock Island." Door County Maritime Museum Lighthouse Walk. 1998.

Karges, Steven. "Sherwood Point Light." Door County Maritime Museum Lighthouse Walk. 1998.

Karges, Steven. "Sturgeon Bay Canal Station Light." Door County Maritime Museum Lighthouse Walk. 1998.

"Kimberly Point Lighthouse Near Completion." *Neenah Daily News-Times*. September 7, 1945.

Koberstein, Paul. "There's a Plan of Action for Fishing Village." *Herald-Times Reporter*. Manitowoc-Two Rivers, WI. August 29, 1979.

Kosich, George. *Beacon of Faith*. November-December 1991.

"Lake Michigan: Friend and Foe." *Ozaukee Press*. September 5, 1985.

Langer, Vivian. "Growing Up at Twin River Point Light Station." *Lighthouse Digest*. Vol. V, No. 2. February, 1996.

Larson, John W. *Those Army Engineers. A History of the Chicago District U.S. Army Corps of Engineers*.

Leberman, J. E. *One Hundred Years of Sheboygan*. 1946.

Lee, John. "Now Outdoors." *The Green Bay Press-Gazette*. July 7, 1974.

Bibliography

LeMay, Konnie. "Are the lights going out?" *Lake Superior Magazine*. Vol. 21, Issue 4. August-September 1999.

Life in a Lighthouse Not One for Sissies. January 22, 1948.

The Light House. *The Weekly Northwestern*. January 8, 1880.

Light List, Volume VII, Great Lakes, 1999. U.S. Department of Transportation. United States Coast Guard.

"Lighthouse Architect Honored." *The Oshkosh Northwestern*. September 22, 1979.

Lighthouse Digest Magazine. June 1999.

"Lighthouse Is Sentinel On Fox River." T*he Oshkosh Northwestern*. 1959.

Light Station. *The Evening Telegram*. Superior, Wisconsin. January 2, 1968.

"Looking Back." *Racine Journal Times*. April 4, 1992.

Mahan, John and Ann. *Wild Lake Michigan*. Voyageur Press. 1991.

McCann, Dennis. "A Spirit of Hope Rises from a Rugged Bit of the State." *Milwaukee Journal Sentinel*. December 14, 1997.

McCann, Dennis. "Bright Beacons." *Milwaukee Journal Sentinel*. May 5, 1996.

McCann, Dennis. "Load Full of Christmas Trees Went Down with the Ship." *Milwaukee Journal Sentinel*. January 11, 1998.

Merkel, Jim. "The Internet: Strengthening the International Community of Lighthouse Lovers." *Lighthouse Digest*. June 1999.

Mersereau, Nancy. "Coast Guard Crew Leaves Shining Lighthouse." *Ozaukee Press*. September 6, 1985.

Metro, Gary."People Positively Wild Over Negative." *Racine Journal Time*s. April 28, 1997.

Milton, Chris. "Life Saving Lights: Cana Island Lighthouse." *Door County Magazin*e. Vol. 3, No. 2, Summer 1999.

Milwaukee Journal Sentinel. November 2, 1998.

Mueller, Theodore. "Sails and Steam on the Milwaukee." *Historical Messenger*. Vol. 10, No. 4, December 1954.

Nenn, Linda. *The History of Port Washington Lighthouses*. 1995.

"New Lighthouse Marks Entrance To Boat Refuge." *The Oshkosh Northwestern*. March 12, 1940.

Noble, Dennis L. and T. Michael O'Brien. *Sentinels of the Rocks*. Northern Michigan University Press. Marquette, Michigan. 1979.

Normyle, Will. "Towering above Lake Michigan Shore, Twin Rivers Light Has Been Ships Guide For 99 Years." *Two Rivers Reporter*. December 12, 1952.

"Oil Burning Beacon atop 1860 Building Was Used to Guide Mariners to Port." *Ozaukee Press*. August 19, 1982.

"Old Lighthouse Tower at Long Tail Built In 1847." *The Green Bay Press-Gazette*. July 18, 1934.

Oleszewski, Wes. *Great Lakes Lighthouses, American and Canadian*. Avery Color Studios, Inc. 1998.

OíMeara, Robert. "Leading Lights." *The Milwaukee Journal*. May 5, 1991.

Penrose, Laurie and Bill Penrose. *A Traveler's Guide to 116 Western Great Lakes Lighthouses*. Friede Publications. 1995.

Pleger, Thomas C. *Green Island Light-Station, Wisconsin. A Synthesis of Related Historical and Archaeological Data*. 1992.

Plesko, Vincent J. "Once Strong against the Elements." *The Evening Telegram*. Superior, Wisconsin. December 4, 1963.

Point Beach State Forest. Wisconsin Department of Natural Resources. Publication PR169.

"Port's Lighthouses: Symbols, Beacons and Welcoming Signs." Ozaukee Press. September 5, 1985.

Program of the Dedication of the Marker for Coast Guard North Point Lighthouse. August 4, 1975.

Putnam, George R. *Lighthouses and Lightships of the United States*. Houghton Mifflin Company. 1933.

Regnier, Kathleen Harris. "Ridges Sanctuary Beginnings Linked to Range Lights." *The Beacon*. Great Lakes Lighthouse Keepers Association. Vol. 14, No. 2, 1996.

Regnier, Kathleen, and Paul. "Life Saving Lights: Baileys Harbor Range Lights." *Door County Magazine.*, Vol. 2, No. 4, Winter 1998-1999.

Report of the Light-House Board, United States Government. 1906.

Roberts, Bruce, and Ray Jones. *Great Lakes Lighthouses*. The Globe Pequot Press. 1994.

Rock Island State Park. Wisconsin Department of Natural Resources Bulletin. 1998.

Rock, Susan. *Potawatomi Lighthouse History*. August 1996.

Rogers St. Fishing Village, *The Quarterly Fishing Village Newsletter*. Volume 1, No. 1. Winter 1991.

Rogers Street Fishing Village, *The Quarterly Fishing Village Newsletter*. Volume 2, No. 2. June 1996.

Ross, Hamilton N. *The Apostle Islands*. 1951.

Rudolph, Jack. *Birthplace of a Commonwealth. A Short History of Brown County, Wisconsin*. Brown County Historical Society. 1976.

Sandin, Jo. "Debate Over Future of Lighthouses Heats Up." *Milwaukee Journal Sentinel*. May 14, 1999.

Schemel, George W. Jr. *Belle City Beacons. Lighthouses of Racine County*. 2nd Edition.

Schoen, Vic. "Lighthouse." *Green Bay Press-Gazette*. April 29, 1984.

Shattuck, S. F. *A History of Neenah*, 1878-1958. 1958.

Sheldon, Bob. "Old Age Catches Up with Reef Lighthouse." *Racine Journal Times*. July 23, 1961

Smith, Jane S. and Michael J. Goc. *Looking Backward, Moving Forward: Ashland, the City of the Garland*. New Past Press Inc. Friendship WI.

"Structure Built by William Bray, Former State Senator, Who Paid Expenses of Keeping It Lighted." *Milwaukee Sentinel*. May 30, 1937.

Surviving Architecture of a Menominee River Boom Town. City of Marinette, Wisconsin. 1990.

"Tiny Bulb Always on Sentry Duty." *Racine Journal Times*. June 25, 1941.

"Tower Nears Completion." *Racine Journal Times*. October 31, 1961.

United States Department of the Interior, National Park Service. Program of Preservation and Utilization. North Point Light Station, Milwaukee, Wisconsin. 1997.

United States Department of the Interior, National Park Service. National Register of Historic Places Inventory-Nomination Form. North Point Light Station, Milwaukee, Wisconsin. 1982.

Van Thiel, John. "Lighthouses—Beacons Light the Passage." *Racine Journal Times*. April 24, 1983.

"Veteran Sailors Declare Winter One of the Hardest in 20 Years." *The Racine Review*. February 8, 1929.

Watson, Bruce. "Science Makes a Better Lighthouse Lens." *Smithsonian*, Volume 30, Number 5. August 1999.

Weade, Sybil. "Life's Lively at Superior Lighthouse." *The Evening Telegram*, Superior, Wisconsin. September 8, 1955.

Bibliography

Werner, Edward C. *Lorinda Merrill, Lighthouse Keeper, July 1871-June 1872*. Kenosha County Historical Society.

Werner, Edward C. *Lighthouse: A History of the Lighthouse at Kenosha (Southport) Wisconsin*. Pike River Graphics, Kenosha. 1990

Wiening, Paul. "Port Washington's Fair Weather Port was Notorious." *Ozaukee Press*. August 19, 1982.

Wind Point Lighthouse. Wind Point Park Board.

Wisconsin Historical Markers.

Wisconsin Trails, vol. 36, no. 5. p. 6. October 1995.

Wisconsin Trails, vol. 39, no. 3. p. 34-41. June 1998.

Wisconsin Trails, vol. 39, no. 4. p. 13. August 1998.

Wright, Larry and Patricia. *Bonfires and Beacons. Great Lakes Lighthouses*. The Boston Mills Press, Ontario. 1996.

Zillier, Carl. "History of Sheboygan County. Wisconsin: Past and Present." Vol 1. 1912

Zorr, Jo. "Lighthouses Remain a Beacon." *The Oshkosh Northwestern*. June 16, 1995.

Additional information on lighthouses may be gathered from these sources.

National Archives
Record Group 26
Washington, DC 20408

U.S. Coast Guard
Historians' Office (G-IP-4)
2100 2nd St., SW
Washington, DC 20593
(202) 267-0948

State Historical Society of Wisconsin
Reference Services
Archives Division
816 State St.
Madison, WI 53706
(608) 264-6400

A wealth of information about lighthouses exists on the Internet. Many of these lighthouse addresses also offer links to other maritime-related subjects.

http://www.ashlandchamber.org Ashland Area Chamber of Commerce, Ashland, WI. 54806
http://www.cr.nps.gov/maritime/
http://www.nps.gov/apis/album.htm
http://www.nps.gov/history/maritime/maripark.html
http://www.state.wi.us/agencies/tourism/guide/reclight.htm
http://www.wisconlin.com/attractions/historic/lighthouses.html
http://www.sealight.com.frsinsde.htm Waddel F. Robey and Aries Knowledge Systems.
http://www.execpc.com/~jeckert/pilot.htm Eckert, Jack A. Life on Pilot Island (circa 1955)

http://www.execpc.com~jeckert/mblh.htm Eckert, Jack A. A Small Slice of Life-Milwaukee Breakwater
Light Station.

http://www.wisconsinwebdesign.com/wmhs/devils.htm Devil's Island Lighthouse.

http://www.uic.edu/~mkoenig/dcmm/light.html

http://www.uscg.mil/general.html

http://www.ipl.org/exhibit/light/

http://www.seagrant.wisc.edu/Communications/Shipwrecks

http://www.execpc.com/~bbaillod

http://sparky.nce.usace.army.mil/COASTAL/lwfacts.htm

http://www.rootsweb.com/~wishboy/

http://www.ais.org/

http://uniontel.net/~cmarlspc/

http://www.usalights.com/lakes.htm

http://www.greatlakeslighthouses.com

http://members.aol.com/uslhswww/lhindex.htm

http://www.ndbc.noaa.gov

http://www.worldlights.com/world

http://wwwlhdigest.com

http://www.lhdepot.com

http://zuma.lib.utk.edu/lights.html

http://www.creative-visions.com/litehse.htm

132

following page: Sherwood Point Lighthouse, Door County